Tomorrow 3.0
Transaction Costs and the Sharing Economy

With the growing popularity of apps such as Uber and Airbnb, there has been a keen interest in the rise of the sharing economy. Michael C. Munger brings these new trends in the economy down to earth by focusing on their relation to the fundamental economic concept of transaction costs. In doing so Munger brings a fresh perspective on the "sharing economy" in clear and engaging writing that is accessible to both general and specialist readers. He shows how, for the first time, entrepreneurs can sell reductions in transaction costs, rather than reductions in the costs of the products themselves. He predicts that smart phones will be used to commodify excess capacity, and reaches the controversial conclusion that a basic income will be required as a consequence of this new "transaction costs revolution."

MICHAEL C. MUNGER is a Professor in the Department of Political Science and the Department of Economics at Duke University. He studied for a PhD under Barry Weingast and Douglass North (1993 Nobel Prize) at Washington University in St. Louis. After working at the US Federal Trade Commission, Munger taught at Dartmouth, Texas, and North Carolina before moving to Duke in 1997. He edited the journal *Public Choice* from 2005 to 2009.

CAMBRIDGE STUDIES IN ECONOMICS, CHOICE, AND SOCIETY

Founding Editors
Timur Kuran, Duke University
Peter J. Boettke, George Mason University

This interdisciplinary series promotes original theoretical and empirical research as well as integrative syntheses involving links between individual choice, institutions, and social outcomes. Contributions are welcome from across the social sciences, particularly in the areas where economic analysis is joined with other disciplines such as comparative political economy, new institutional economics, and behavioral economics.

Books in the Series

TERRY L. ANDERSON and GARY D. LIBECAP *Environmental Markets: A Property Rights Approach*

MORRIS B. HOFFMAN *The Punisher's Brain: The Evolution of Judge and Jury*

PETER T. LEESON *Anarchy Unbound: Why Self-Governance Works Better Than You Think*

BENJAMIN POWELL *Out of Poverty: Sweatshops in the Global Economy*

CASS R. SUNSTEIN *The Ethics of Influence: Government in the Age of Behavioral Science*

JARED RUBIN *Rulers, Religion, and Riches: Why the West Got Rich and the Middle East Did Not*

JEAN-PHILIPPE PLATTEAU *Islam Instrumentalized: Religion and Politics in Historical Perspective*

TAIZU ZHANG *The Laws and Economics of Confucianism: Kinship and Property in Preindustrial China and England*

ROGER KOPPL *Expert Failure*

CAROLYN M. WARNER, RAMAZAN KILINÇ, CHRISTOPHER W. HALE, and ADAM B. COHEN *Generating Generosity in Catholicism and Islam: Beliefs, Institutions, and Public Goods Provision*

Tomorrow 3.0

Transaction Costs and the Sharing Economy

MICHAEL C. MUNGER
Duke University

CAMBRIDGE
UNIVERSITY PRESS

CAMBRIDGE
UNIVERSITY PRESS

University Printing House, Cambridge CB2 8BS, United Kingdom

One Liberty Plaza, 20th Floor, New York, NY 10006, USA

477 Williamstown Road, Port Melbourne, VIC 3207, Australia

314–321, 3rd Floor, Plot 3, Splendor Forum, Jasola District Centre, New Delhi – 110025, India

79 Anson Road, #06–04/06, Singapore 079906

Cambridge University Press is part of the University of Cambridge.

It furthers the University's mission by disseminating knowledge in the pursuit of education, learning, and research at the highest international levels of excellence.

www.cambridge.org
Information on this title: www.cambridge.org/9781108427081
DOI: 10.1017/9781108602341

© Michael C. Munger 2018

First published 2018

Printed in the United States of America by Sheridan Books, Inc.

A catalogue record for this publication is available from the British Library.

ISBN 978-1-108-42708-1 Hardback
ISBN 978-1-108-44734-8 Paperback

Cambridge University Press has no responsibility for the persistence or accuracy of URLs for external or third-party internet websites referred to in this publication and does not guarantee that any content on such websites is, or will remain, accurate or appropriate.

To Donna Gingerella,
who showed me how to love,
&
to Skippy Squirrelbane,
who showed me how to live

No one claimed that any of their possessions was their own, but they shared everything they had.

Acts 4:32

Contents

Preface

There is a lovely apocryphal story, generally told about Dwight
D. Eisenhower during his time as president of Columbia University:
The school was growing, necessitating an expansion of the campus, which
produced a very hot dispute between two groups of planners and
architects about where the sidewalks should go. One camp insisted that
it was obvious – self-evident! – that the sidewalks had to be arranged thus,
as any rational person could see, while the other camp argued for
something very different, with the same appeals to obviously,
self-evident, rational evidence. Legend has it that Eisenhower solved the
problem by ordering that the sidewalks not be laid down at all for a year:
The students would trample paths in the grass, and the builders would
then pave over where the students were actually walking. Neither of the
plans that had been advocated matched what the students actually did
when left to their own devices. There are two radically different ways of
looking at the world embedded in that story: Are our institutions here
to tell us where to go, or are they here to help smooth the way for us as we
pursue our own ends, going our own ways?

Kevin Williamson, 2013

The story above is true, even though it likely never happened.
The "truth" lies in its core insight that permissionless innovation is,
or should be, what institutions seek to promote. As Lu Xun put
succinctly: "Originally there was no path – yet, as people are walking
all the time in the same spot, a way appears."

There is a simple logic to the "way" that is appearing all around
us: reduced *transactions costs* foster *permissionless innovation* to
make more efficient use of *excess capacity*. The result is that more
people can get cheaper, better access to the stuff we already have.
Markets are, or *can* be, a form of sharing, because people often just
want to use things, not (necessarily) to own them. This has always
been true to some extent – I never owned the huge factory machines

that made my clothing; I simply shared them for a few seconds at some point, and then gave them back – but the rate of change and the expansion of sharing today is unprecedented. If you want to know why at present we own rather than share, the answer is transaction costs. And that is all going to change.

THE ARGUMENT

A simple summary of an entire book can be misleading because it is simple, and a summary, and therefore leaves out both details and the steps in the argument. Nonetheless, it is worthwhile to provide a map, if only to help the reader identify where each step in the larger argument is located in the hilly terrain to come.

The history of growth, and destruction, in economics has centered on complex voluntary interdependencies caused by the division of labor and specialization. I can produce far more widgets if I do nothing but practice my widget-making skills, while you produce corn, and Jones over there produces only clothing. There is lots more stuff in the world if each of us specializes, but we will only do that if we can rely on being able to acquire, by exchange or some other form of cooperative sharing, the stuff we ourselves do not produce. Until recently, much of this specialization has centered on skills in production and finding ways to make more stuff.

But now that is changing. In the past 20 years – dating the change roughly from eBay's expansion in 1997, after beginning as "AuctionWeb" in 1995 – entrepreneurs have for the first time been able to specialize in selling not more stuff, but reductions in transaction costs for access to existing stuff. One could argue, with some merit, that the oldest organizations that specialized solely in selling reductions in transaction costs were marketplaces, or "Souqs," in northern Africa and western Asia. Until the recent disastrous events in Syria, the al-Madina Souq in Aleppo had been open for business for well over 4,000 years.

The al-Madina is a (partly) covered area that extends over 10 kilometers in terms of the storefronts and open-air stalls that open

onto streets and alleys. You can find almost anything there.
The reason merchants sell there is that they know you can find other
things there as well. That does not seem to make sense: it seems like
merchants would want to be off by themselves, far from any
competition. Why would a fruit merchant want to be in a place where
there are hundreds of other fruit merchants? The answer is
transaction costs: gathering many sellers into one large physical
area reduces the effort required for "comparison shopping" for
customers.

The notion of a "market" as a means of reducing transaction
costs long meant a physical place where people knew to gather to buy
and sell. But one thing that the Sears catalog was clearly selling was a
reduction in transaction costs: farmers in rural areas who might not
otherwise have access to any specialized products could, if they
waited a couple of months, obtain from Sears anything from clothing
to food preparation tools to cars or houses. Sellers of commodities
contacted Sears (as they now contact Amazon) to list their products
for sale, gathering in a "place" that was in a sense virtual rather than
real. Of course, the virtual space was not online but lived in the pages
of a thick catalog. Still, that was the place to go. So while the
differences I am talking about are real, there are plenty of examples in
the past if you know where to look.

And that is the key to understanding the contribution of this
book: the sustained thesis is that the single key fact in explaining the
disruption of the economic system in the past 20 years or so is the
sharp reduction in the transaction costs of commodifying many things
that we have never before thought of as commodities. Lower
transaction costs facilitate a hybrid form of "collaborative
consumption." If you own something, you can extract some of this
unused value by renting it out. If you own almost nothing, you can
still enjoy much of the value of ownership by renting from someone
else. But this more intensive use of existing resources can only happen
if transaction costs – the sum of what I will call triangulation, transfer,
and trust – convert unused stuff into usable excess capacity. To make

a long story short, both the sharing economy and the middleman economy are *sort of* new, but only in intensity and rapidity of change.

That does not mean that reducing transaction costs has never been important before. To the contrary, reducing transaction costs has been an important source of creating value since the very first transactions. After all, "length of braided vines three miles away, across a mountain" is much less valuable than "length of braided vines in my hand, ready to use to tie bundle of wood." So a crucial part of transactions, and in fact an essential part of the competition to sell things, has always been the transaction costs. The reason is that, to consumers, all costs are transaction costs. Reducing the cost of physical production by 10 percent is no different from reducing the cost of delivery and convenience of use by 10 percent, from the point of view of the consumer.

Consequently, economists have long highlighted reductions in transaction costs as a focus of economic innovation and competition. Joseph Schumpeter (1934; 66) listed "types" or categories of innovations that entrepreneurs focused on, and transaction costs are important aspects of three of them:

(1) a new good, or an old good with a qualitatively different level of quality
(2) a new technique for producing or handling the product
(3) the opening of a new market, or recognition of a new use for the product
(4) improvements in security or reductions in costs of raw materials or partly-manufactured goods up the supply chain
(5) the conception and execution of a new system or organization for manufacturing or delivering the good.

But Schumpeter saw the transaction costs elements as something that helped the entrepreneur sell the *product*, though to his credit he recognized that low transaction costs were an essential part of the product themselves.

This theme of institutional innovation and the form of delivery and measurement was echoed by other economists, including Commons (1931) and Chandler (1977). But for the most part – there are exceptions, such as firms that specialize in accounting audits or management consulting – the innovations in transaction costs were attached to a product or service. What has happened in the last 20 years is that many firms simply offer to sell reductions in transaction costs without knowing what products or services will be sold as a result.

That means that what we are seeing are the early signs of a revolution being driven along two quite different dimensions. The intersection of these dimensions explains the growth of the new economy to date; where they are far apart, we learn why many sectors are yet unaffected.

The two dimensions are (1) the sharing economy and (2) the transaction costs or middleman economy.

The *sharing economy* is

(1) entrepreneurship applied to reducing transaction costs rather than reducing production costs
(2) working through new software platforms
(3) operating on smart, portable hardware
(4) connected over the web.

Software programs in the sharing economy are both system (executing instructions) and application (storing, retrieving, and interpreting information entered by users). Software will play the same role in producing reductions in transaction costs that robots and automation have played in reduction production costs in the ownership economy. Software will displace human workers, reducing both actual prices and implicit costs, and expanding the set of things that we think of as commodities.

The *middleman economy* arises from the ability to sell reductions in transaction costs to enable mutually beneficial exchange in commodities, services, and activities that may not even have been conceived as commercial until now.

This means that there are two variables of concern: excess capacity and transaction costs. Excess capacity is the unused time or space to do more. Excess capacity is expensive, but we may not notice the cost because it can only be measured by things not done. Transaction costs are the expenses, including time, inconvenience, and actual payments required to use the item, and the problems involved in trusting others to deliver on their promises and not to rob us.

The value proposition in the new economy is selling access to excess capacity. As transaction costs are driven by new software applications, it is more expensive to hold or store consumer and producer durables, precisely because new software applications makes it cheaper to use them.

My storage unit, my garage, my kitchen cupboards, and my closets are all full of useful stuff. I am not using them; in fact, I am paying to store them. But in many cases, someone *else* would pay to use them. Excess capacity of durable goods is variable with respect to the transaction cost – triangulation, transfer, and trust – of reassigning their temporary use.

Of course, when I look at my closet or garage, I do not see "excess capacity," I see storage of valuable items. But those suits, shirts, my car, my mower, all those things could be being used by someone else. Lowering transaction costs raises the opportunity cost of idle durable goods. Still, that does not translate into "excess capacity" until we found a way of selling reductions in transaction costs.

And now, because of the combination of portable smart communication devices, a set of software apps that run on those devices, and a network to connect those devices, we have found a way. That is why tomorrow will be different.

Acknowledgments

This book grew out of a conversation I had with Russ Roberts on his podcast show, *EconTalk*, in 2014. Our discussion was so interesting that I realized there were big holes in the way that I thought about the developing economy in which sharing excess capacity and mobile apps selling reductions in transaction costs were going to transform the world. In writing the book, I have received helpful comments and suggestions from thousands of people, in conversations and seminars in Australia, Austria, Canada, Chile, Czech Republic, France, Germany, Slovakia, and at least two dozen colleges, universities, and professional meetings in the United States. Thanks to all of you who suffered through the early versions, and my apologies for not being able to implement all of your great ideas.

There are a number of people who made very extensive and detailed comments. I have likely forgotten some. But at a minimum, thanks to Jonathan Anomaly, Petr Barton, Darren Beatty, Philip Booth, Sam Bowman, Paul Burgess, Bruce Caldwell, Arthur Carden, Carlos Carvalho, Scott de Marchi, Richard Durana, Michael A. Gillespie, Kevin Grier, Daniel Gropper, Victoria Heid, Susan Hogarth, Libby Jenke, Clemens Kauffmann, Lynne Kiesling, Jason McDonald, Kevin Munger, Yaël Ossowski, Richard Salsman, Josef Sima, Ed Tower, John Transue, Mario Villareal-Diaz, Roy Weintraub, and Stan Winer. Curtis Brim of Duke University's Political Science Department made numerous suggestions on content, and was primarily responsible for preparing the index. Margaret Puskar-Pasewicz edited the prose into something closer to English, and was cheerful about some difficult deadlines. And thanks to Peter Boettke and Timur Kuran, editors of the Cambridge University Press series, "Cambridge Studies in Economics, Choice, and Society," as well as the anonymous reviewers and the production staff at Cambridge University Press, who managed to handle everything remarkably efficiently. Finally, thanks to Shaun King and the folks who lent their arms for the cover. Several people have asked "Why are there no 'persons of color' in the photo?" Don't be so sure. Seeing everything in black and white makes you miss the shades.

1   The World of Tomorrow 3.0

To summarize the summary of the summary: people are a problem.

Douglas Adams, *The Restaurant at the End of the Universe* (1980)

I need to drive screws in some wood furniture I'm assembling. I open an app on my smart phone and tell the app "rent drill." A car – I don't know where it is and I don't need to – picks up a drill that matches my pre-programmed preferences from a hardware store. The car delivers it to a security-coded pod outside my apartment. My phone vibrates: "drill delivered." I assemble the furniture and return the drill to the pod. The pod is smart: its software is connected through the "Internet of Things," and the pod tells another car – no particular car, just whomever is nearby, according to the software – that there is a pick-up.

The rental costs me $2.50 and no more than a minute spent shopping, obtaining, and retrieving the drill. I got brief access (but that's all I needed!) to a commercial quality power tool. It could have been a saw, a fruit dehydrator, a bread machine, a deep fryer, a sausage grinder, or a collapsible bar to serve drinks at a party. There are few cupboards or closets in my apartment and no parking spaces on the street outside. All the space is used for people, instead of stuff. I own almost nothing, yet have immediate access to everything. Amazon is now a *software* company; Uber is now the main provider of rental services, delivered by *software*-directed driverless cars. The work week is only two days long. But many people have no "job," in the traditional sense, at all. Wages have fallen dramatically, for most people. On the other hand, prices have fallen by even more, and many prices are near zero because society now shares so many products.

What happened? This is Tomorrow, 3.0. It's what the economy looks like after the third great economic revolution. The first was the

Neolithic; the second was the Industrial Revolution. Look around you. The third revolution has already begun.

THE TRANSACTION COST REVOLUTION

People own stuff. In the developed world, they own *so much* stuff. The self-storage industry in the US has nearly 50,000 facilities, with more than 15 billion cubic feet of space cluttered with stuff (Clark, 2014). We store bicycles, furniture, appliances, and electronics in metal boxes that are more solidly constructed, and more expensive, than the average *human* habitation in many developing nations.

Why? Fifty years from now people will look back on this era and be amazed at our selfishness. Why would we *store* stuff rather than let other people *use* it? Why would we store that stuff in our houses, or in parking garages, or spaces on busy streets? It would seem that our own selfishness should have led us to want less stuff so we could have more space.

The answer is surprisingly simple: what looks like selfishness is just a consequence of *transaction costs*.[1] In the next chapter, I'll explain in more detail what that means. But for now, the important thing is just that we have stuff, and we store stuff, because doing anything else is more trouble than it's worth. If I own something, I control it. If I want to rent, or borrow that thing, I'm much more dependent on other people.

Still, when you think about it, people don't fundamentally want *stuff*. What they want is the *stream of services* that stuff provides, over time. So, if people *own* stuff – clothes, tools, cars, houses – rather than *rent*, it is because owning secures services more reliably and at lower cost than renting. But this "preference" for owning is not

---

[1] The literature on "transaction costs" is large. Key contributions include Coase (1937, 1960), Demsetz (1966, 1969), North (1981, 1990), and Williamson (1975, 1985). A particularly important but under-recognized contribution is Graham, et al. (1972), who recognize the contingent optimality of equilibria in the presence of transaction costs.

real. It could change quickly, if entrepreneurs can figure out ways to *sell reductions in transaction costs*.

And that, in a nutshell, is the thesis of this book: until now, to make money people have had to make, and sell, *stuff*. They often found ways to reduce the transaction costs of those sales, but it was primarily in service of selling the stuff. From now on, much of the new value in the economy is going to come from creating and selling reductions in transaction costs, making better use of stuff that already exists. That change will redefine of our deepest ideas of "commodity," because almost anything could in principle be rented.

We Are Already the Cooperators We Need to Be

Adam Smith famously said that human beings have a "disposition to truck, barter, and exchange" (Smith, 1981, p. 14).[2] All of these are forms of cooperation and sharing, and they take advantage of the fact that we are all different. Instead of taking by force, we negotiate and try to figure out ways that both of us can be better off. We have enough stuff, but it's in the wrong places. If we share, even just by exchanging stuff we already have, many things will move to higher-valued uses.

It might seem like the fact that we are different might make it harder to share, not easier. But in many cases our very dissimilarities are a source of cooperation and benefits from exchange. Say you are

---

[2] "By nature a philosopher is not in genius and disposition half so different from a street porter, as a mastiff is from a greyhound, or a greyhound from a spaniel, or this last from a shepherd's dog. [But] the strength of the mastiff is not in the least supported either by the swiftness of the greyhound, or by the sagacity of the spaniel, or by the docility of the shepherd's dog. The effects of those different geniuses and talents, for want of the power or disposition to barter and exchange, cannot be brought into a common stock, and do not in the least contribute to the better accommodation and conveniency of the species ... and derives no sort of advantage from that variety of talents with which nature has distinguished its fellows. Among men, on the contrary, the most dissimilar geniuses are of use to one another; the different produces of their respective talents, by the general disposition to truck, barter, and exchange, being brought, as it were, into a common stock, where every man may purchase whatever part of the produce of other men's talents he has occasion for." See Smith (1981, pp. 14).

good at farming, and I'm good at fishing. We can both be better off if we specialize. These talents need not be innate (though they could be). The important thing is that, through taste, talent, or practice, you are better – at something – than I am. That means that I'm better off trading with you than trying to do everything for myself.

This requires cooperation. But cooperativeness is the *default*, the core tendency, the central psychological fact of human society. Some arrangements called "markets" nurture and expand this natural cooperativeness, at least under some circumstances. In a functioning market, I don't need to know how to do *everything* because I can hire others who have acquired knowledge through practice or ingenuity. This willingness to depend on others creates enormous potential benefits, as all of us work for everybody else. But there is sand in the gears of the system: transaction costs. Transaction costs prevent cooperation, even if that cooperation would be mutually beneficial.

In particular, transaction costs prevent exchanges that would otherwise make two or more people better off. That may not seem so important, but it is. Exchanges correct "mistakes," because resources are usually not being used in the most valuable way. The reasons may be complicated, involving history, accident, and the residue of dynamic change: what once was optimal is now anachronistic. But that means that people are holding onto resources that other people need more, simply because of transaction costs. If transactions costs can be reduced, people will be able to specialize: each of us can own just a few things, and rent those out to others when we aren't using them. And we can rent the things that someone else has "specialized" in.

For example: I have three old bicycles in my garage. Those bikes have been there for years, unused. That's not just an inefficient use of resources; it's also selfish, maybe even immoral. I could have allowed someone who values those bikes to use them, as long as it didn't cost me anything. Am I a pathetic miser, counting unused bikes and chortling gleefully at my treasure hoard, a low-rent Smaug?

No. The problem is transaction costs. I cannot cheaply or easily find someone who wants to use the bike. So the services of the bike are wasted, but there is no obvious way of making better use of them. I could probably find someone who wanted to use one of the bikes for an hour, or a day. But they wouldn't pay much for that, and I wouldn't be sure I could trust them to return the bike. And it would all be a lot of trouble. So there they sit.

Once you understand transaction costs, it will change the way you think about almost everything. If I need my yard mowed and the leaves blown, why don't I hire the man in Chowmuhani, or the man in Ambohitompoina, either of whom would gladly do the work for $5 per day? It wouldn't be exploitative; these workers would love to have the job because they are only making $3 per day at present. Still, the answer makes the question seem silly: Chowmuhani is in Bangladesh, and Ambohitompoina is in Madagascar. The costs of finding that willing worker, agreeing on a price, transporting him physically to my leaf-choked yard in North Carolina, and then monitoring his work dwarfs the amount I can pay. Those three costs – which I will call triangulation, transfer, and trust – ensure that the world economy is full of mistakes: *resources should move*, but they don't.

THE THIRD GREAT ECONOMIC REVOLUTION: WHY OWN WHEN YOU COULD RENT?

Suellentrop (2010, p. 33) claimed, in a way that now looks prescient, "We woke up in a Rentership Society, and it's starting to look permanent. And you know what? Thank goodness. Ownership, it turns out, is for suckers."

If you own something, you have to pay the *average* cost of using it because no one can share it, and you have to pay for what it costs to create and store that thing. If I own a flat, I'm already paying for utilities and making mortgage payments. But what if I'm not always there, or if I have an extra room I only use to store junk? I would be willing – maybe even happy – to offer someone else my place to stay at the cost of having to clean it afterwards, plus whatever extra I can get to pay toward my rent. This cost of use is called *marginal* cost, the expense of sharing the unit for one period of time. If I can collect enough to pay my marginal cost, plus part of my mortgage, for a week that I'm going to be away anyway, I'm ahead. If you come to my city, I'd be willing to rent you a room, provided we can solve the transaction cost problem of triangulation, transfer, and trust.[3]

Likewise, I'm willing to offer rides in my car at the cost of gas, my time, and wear and tear on the vehicle – the *marginal* cost – if I can also make *some* of the car payment for that month, reducing the amount I have to pay out of my pocket. I don't have to make enough to cover the entire car payment, like a taxi driver would. I just need to cover some of it. If I have a car and a few minutes, I have some excess capacity. If you need a ride, there may well be a way for us to share.

The reason we don't see more sharing is that the three components of transaction costs are so hard to negotiate. As I outlined earlier, these include:

Triangulation information about identity and location, and agreeing on terms, including price

Transfer a way of transferring payment and good that is immediate and as invisible as possible

Trust a way of outsourcing assurance of honesty and performance of the terms of the contract.

The problem isn't new of course, but this approach to thinking of everything in terms of transaction costs may take a little getting

---

[3] This difference between "marginal" and "average" costs has important implications. If you go to a resort town, perhaps at the beach in New England, and stop at a restaurant in January, you notice that you are the only customer at 12:30 pm. And you ask yourself, "How can this place stay open? It's totally dead around here." The answer is that the restaurant has many fixed costs, such as rent and utilities (they have to keep the heat on, so the pipes don't freeze!). They have to pay those costs regardless of whether they open for business or not. The marginal costs, the costs of opening for business, are just the costs of food, the wages of the cook and service staff, and some electricity for the sign out front that says "OPEN." If the restaurant can cover the marginal costs, plus even just a small part of their average costs, they are ahead. They aren't making money, but they are losing less than if they stayed closed. Uber operates on the same principle: drivers don't have to make their full car payment in fares to make it useful to drive for money, as long as they cover their marginal costs. Rifkin (2014) questions whether traditional models of capitalist markets can survive the move to marginal cost pricing, or whether some other form of "collaborative sharing" will replace it.

used to. We can use transaction costs to explain things you may have taken for granted. Consider this: if you are going to a city where you don't know anyone, where will you stay? In principle that seems like a hard problem. In fact, it's easy: you stay in a hotel, an organization that has specialized in owning rooms that it can rent out.

But which hotel? To solve that problem, we use a solution called *brand name*. Brand names solve all three transaction costs problems. Still, hotels are expensive because they have to cover their *average* costs: all their value is in the business of selling rooms by the night. Hotels have to charge enough to cover all their mortgage, utilities, the upkeep of their buildings, and wages to employees. That's not true of apartments or homes where people live because those other expenses are being paid already. If I can make even a little money off the apartment where I live, it's all extra cash. So I can charge a price that covers just my additional costs and still be glad to have access to the transaction.

That low price will be better for the buyer also, of course, as long as the three categories of transaction costs can be reliably reduced. A company called Airbnb figured this out. In fact, Airbnb does not rent out space; it sells (1) information on availability and location (triangulation), (2) reliable transactions clearing, and (3) "distributed trust," or dependable access to vetted market participants, so that trustworthy buyers find trustworthy sellers. The rest is up to the people who have stuff (in this case, space) and the people who want to rent that stuff (in this case, an accommodation in a place where they don't know anyone but want to sleep safely).

There is an alternative, and even more extreme, form of "renting" that may be of great importance within a decade or less. That would be "renting" the particular form in which pellets or filament have been "printed" by a 3D printer. If the speed and value of 3D printing continue to increase, and if the cost of reducing the material at the end of its desired use is low enough, then all that would be necessary is to "rent" the material in a particular printed form for a small amount of time. The "buyer" could have the device delivered, and then return it to the 3D print shop, where it would be reduced to its constituent metal and plastic parts and used again. Of course, if this scenario comes to fruition it will mean that no one may need to own any tools at all. It would also mean that there would be no manufacturing at all: presumably, 3D printers should be able to print 3D printers. I will not say much about this possibility because a lot of things would have to be worked out before such a system could function.

The point is that, regardless of whether the simple or the extreme form of "renting" comes to dominate, overall each of us will have far fewer actual possessions while we make better use of the stuff we still have. We'll be less selfish, less crowded, richer, and more cooperative, all because entrepreneurs can sell reductions in transaction costs.

SOFTWARE EATS THE WORLD

The quote I used to start this chapter sounded pessimistic: "People are a problem." But people *want* to cooperate. The reason people are a problem is that transaction costs can prevent us from helping each other. But increasingly entrepreneurs can use software to reduce transaction costs so other people can share. Software is the "robot" of exchange: where automation replaces humans in manufacturing, software automates *transactions*.

What changed? Two things came together, and a third thing caught up. First, the Internet was constructed, providing very cheap pathways for communication and allowing "permissionless innovation" (more on that later). Second, hardware platforms, particularly smartphones, allowed universal, portable, continuous access to the Internet. The thing that "caught up" was the developing world: suddenly the source of labor for entrepreneurship, and the focus of value-creating exchange, exploded from the 2 billion people in the "first world" to more than 7 billion people, all over the world. Distance, borders, and language are all transaction costs barriers, but with smart phones connected to the Internet they are much less important.

With that platform and those connections, the number and variety of software applications exploded. Marc Andreessen saw it clearly in 2011:

More and more major businesses and industries are being run on software and delivered as online services – from movies to agriculture to national defense. Many of the winners are Silicon Valley-style entrepreneurial technology companies that are invading and overturning established industry structures. Over the next 10 years, I expect many more industries to be disrupted by software, with new world-beating Silicon Valley companies doing the disruption in more cases than not.

Andreessen connected several apparently unrelated events: many things, of many different kinds that had once been done for pay by humans are now done nearly for free by software. Not robots, *software*. But more than that, software can do – and in some cases is already doing – new things humans have *never done*, and have *never thought of doing* because until now the transaction costs have been too high.

In a way, there's nothing new here. Specialization has always meant that people have to solve the problem of cooperating in groups, and larger groups create much larger transaction costs. Over and over again, independently in societies without social contact, people came up with almost exactly the same solution: the original "software" – money.

Money stands in – at one remove – for actual value. Aristotle recognized this as a crucial step in the evolution of a market society.[4]

---

[4] Aristotle's view is quite nuanced:

> In the [household] there is no function for trade, but it only arises after the association has become more numerous. For the members of the primitive household used to share commodities that were all their own, whereas on the contrary a group divided into several households participated also in a number of commodities belonging to their neighbors, according to their needs for which they were forced to make their interchanges by way of barter, as also many barbarian tribes do still; for such tribes do not go beyond exchanging actual commodities for actual commodities.
>
> ... [W]hen they had come to supply themselves more from abroad by importing things in which they were deficient and exporting those of which they had a surplus, the employment of money necessarily came to be devised. For the natural necessaries are not in every case readily portable; hence for the purpose of barter men made a mutual compact to give and accept some substance of such a sort as being

He describes a "stamp" as standing in for actual commodities. That stamp is *software*: A set of instructions that direct a computer. Aristotle's trading stamp was a crude analog computer, but a computer nonetheless. The symbol on paper signified value, but it also created value, in the sense that it sharply reduced the transaction costs of exchange compared to barter.[5] The "instruction" was the number on the stamp: larger numbers meant more value, even the paper and the number had no intrinsic value at all; it was just an instruction, a mark on a preserving, communicable medium. The "computers" are the minds of human beings, which process transactions in markets using that software.

Currency allows "value" to be reduced to an abstract concept, rather than requiring the cumbersome transfer of the physical commodities that the stamp represented. The fact that people *want* to be able to exchange – the only way I can be better off is if I find a way to make you better off – is not enough. They have to find a way to reduce transactions cost below the value being produced by the exchange, or the exchange won't happen.

Many, many potentially beneficial acts of cooperation don't happen. *Each one* of us, on a planet of nearly 7.5 billion people, is wasting time and storage space. Every minute of every day there is *something* we are willing to do that would benefit someone else a great deal. The same is true of many of the things we own, work with, and see around us: someone, somewhere, wants that thing more than we want it. But we don't know they need it and they don't know we have it.[6]

---

itself a useful commodity was easy to handle in use for general life, iron for instance, silver and other metals, at the first stage defined merely by size and weight, but finally also by impressing on it a stamp in order that this might relieve them of having to measure it; *for the stamp was put on as a token of the amount.*

(Aristotle, Politics, *Book I, Section 1257a; emphasis added*)

[5] The most interesting and wide-ranging history of money and the notions of using abstract value on notes issued by private entities (which might be, but would not have to be, banks) is Selgin and White (1994).

[6] F. A. Hayek (1945, p. 520) calls attention to the pervasiveness of this general problem of lacking "the knowledge of the particular circumstances of time and place."

In economic terms, inputs and labor "want" to be more productive, to find higher-valued uses. But in terms of actual agency that's no more true than saying that giraffes "want" to have long necks. The active agent in biological evolution is natural selection; the active agent in economics is entrepreneurship. Entrepreneurs relentlessly seeking profits search for resources that can be moved, transformed, or combined in ways that can be sold at a profit.

Armen Alchian (1950) famously argued that it need not be true that firms and managers all "want" to make profits. They may want a variety of things, and some organizations may not want any one thing at all. But once the selection mechanism – profits must be positive, for the firm to survive –, eliminates all the firms that are losing money, it will look as if firms are *seeking* profits. This means that no one – including entrepreneurs – may actually know in advance what kind of transaction costs reductions will create profits and new transactions.

But constant trial and error, and low-cost "permissionless innovation" resulting from the writing of new smart phone "apps" will be a very efficient means of searching the space of possibly profitable opportunities. As Alchian put it, the problem is that when "foresight is uncertain, [optimization] is meaningless as a guide to specifiable action ... Uncertainty arises from at least two sources: imperfect foresight and human inability to solve complex problems containing a host of variables even when an optimum is definable" (1950, pp. 211–212). The point is not that entrepreneurs know *which* software will eat the world; they don't know any more than the rest of us. But with so many people writing software, most of it terrible, some will get lucky and create an app that many people want to use.

Markets "want" to move assets and services toward higher-valued uses; transaction costs act like friction in an engine, reducing power and efficiency while producing nothing but heat. Of course, if entrepreneurship is ubiquitous, the particular effects on the economy must be filtered through institutions, or the rules, property rights structures, and incentives that are socially constructed and enforced (Boettke and Coyne, 2003, 2009).

In the early dawn of the Industrial Revolution, in 1740, the Scottish philosopher David Hume speculated on the problem of cooperation, in a world where we are dependent on each other, and yet people are a problem. He said,

> Of all the animals, with which this globe is peopled, there is none towards whom nature seems, at first sight, to have exercis'd more cruelty than towards man, in the numberless wants and necessities, with which she has loaded him, and in the slender means, which she affords to the relieving these necessities.
>
> ... 'Tis by society alone he is able to supply his defects, and raise himself up to an equality with his fellow-creatures, and even acquire a superiority above them. By society all his infirmities are compensated... When every individual person labours a-part, and only for himself, his force is too small to execute any considerable work; his labour being employ'd in supplying all his different necessities, he never attains a perfection in any particular art; and as his force and success are not at all times equal, the least failure in either of these particulars must be attended with inevitable ruin and misery.
>
> ... [But] by the partition of employments, our ability encreases: And by mutual succour we are less expos'd to fortune and accidents.' Tis by this additional force, ability, and security, that society becomes advantageous.
>
> *(Hume, 2004, Part II, Section 2)*

The problem Hume identifies is that we all depend on "society," but society is not actually any one thing that you can point to or direct. Society is the aggregate consequence of many individual actions that are not planned or centrally directed. And people are a problem: as he says later on the same page, we are not innately "sensible of these advantages" of being dependent on society. Further, the great convulsions of economic revolutions can be destructive of the relations in society that we do cultivate.

So, while the prospect of "software eats the world" seems distressing, we have been here before. In the Industrial Revolution, a steampunk Marc Andreessen might have said, "Division of labor eats the world." And he would have been right. A few workers in Lancashire, England, using Crompton's "Spinning Mule," could produce far more cloth than hundreds of workers sitting at hand looms. And the cloth was stronger and softer, ensuring that even the poor could afford clothing of a quality that would have been out of the reach of all but the wealthiest elite just half a century earlier.

That's all good, if you are a consumer: much cheaper cloth and much better clothing. But hundreds of thousands of *workers* lost their jobs worldwide.[7] Their jobs were not "shipped overseas"; the productivity increases resulting from division of labor were eating the world. Capitalism is a system based on *consumer* sovereignty, animated by the responses of owners of resources to prices, and by entrepreneurs to prospects of profit and loss. Capitalism does not "produce" jobs; it usually destroys them.

The observation that workers would lose their jobs to increased productivity spurred Karl Marx to prophesy that real wages – what workers' pay will actually *buy* – would be driven down as labor was ground up in the relentless machine-like gears of increased productivity. The opposite turned out to be true: prices fell dramatically, but nominal wages *rose* with productivity. Rising nominal wages and falling prices imply a skyrocketing real wage, for much of the world, for much of the time since 1750. It's not just clothing; almost every material aspect of life – for consumers – is now far better, more affordable, with more choices and better quality.[8] Far more jobs were

---

[7] "Hundreds of thousands" may be conservative. And the effects were complex. For a fascinating and nuanced description of the effects of the Industrial Revolution in England, see Griffin (2014), especially chapters 1 and 2.

[8] This is true for even the poorest members of society, as innovations that start out as very expensive quickly become mass-produced at prices that fall by 90 percent or more. The first "home" computers cost $30,000 in current dollars. DVD players and HD televisions have fallen in price by more than 90 percent in real terms since they were introduced. And of course, smart phones and Facebook didn't exist. Not all products make it, of course. The original "Google Glass" was expensive ($1,500 each) and was never mass-produced. The Apple "Newton" cost $2,000 in today's dollars, and was discontinued because no one wanted to pay that much. But MP3 players

created than were destroyed, as wealth creation fed back on itself in the form of creation of new capital and a need for more educated workers, who in turn were more productive and earned far higher salaries.

Will it happen again? The new value proposition for the production of economic surplus is using software platforms to sell reductions in transaction costs. What are the implications of this change? Where will the new jobs come from this time?

REIMAGINING PRODUCTION – EXCESS CAPACITY *WANTS* TO BE USED

Until now, the drive to reduce transactions costs has been in service of selling new production. Reducing transaction costs has been important because that allows lower delivered prices to consumers. But only in a few instances – the auction houses, such as Christie's or Sotheby's, come to mind – has anyone tried to sell reductions in transactions costs in the abstract.

Consider a souq, in western Asia, or a flea market, or an auction session at Sotheby's. There are few restrictions on who can sell or what can be sold; the sellers just pay a fee to owners of the venue and then try to find buyers. Of course, the reason that it's worth paying a fee is that sellers know that buyers know these are the places to go. It would be much more difficult to wander around the city as a buyer looking for isolated carts selling things, and the carts themselves wouldn't sell enough to make it worth even going to the city in the first place.

These kinds of "markets" are physical spaces. We could take one step away and use bulletin boards or classified ads in newspapers to advertise: "I have this, I am in this location, and my price is

---

have fallen in price from more than $500 (current dollars) for a MPMan F10 to less than $50, for a product with more than 1,000 times as much storage capacity. (The MPMan F10 had 32 MB of space, enough to hold perhaps ten normal songs, or an album, if anyone remembers albums).

this much." Then the "place" is not physical, but the newspaper can charge a fee because sellers know that buyers know they can find useful things in the want ads.

In a sense, that's all eBay ever was, a virtual or online collection of want ads. But the fact that you can search for anything you want means that you may be able to sell almost anything you want. As Anderson (2008) notes in his description of "The Long Tail," reducing the costs of making exotic things available mean that sellers no longer need to concentrate on high volume items.

Of course, buying and selling used stuff is not the same as "sharing." Where does the sharing part of the sharing economy come in? Open source software exemplifies the idea of an infinitely shareable product at very low cost.

That is, it's the software itself, the actual code, that is being shared. Investigating the history of open source illustrates some of the problems and paradoxes at work. It's worth a diversion.

Real Sharing: Open Source

One of the urtexts of the history of open source software is Philip Elmer-Dewitt's article, "Computers: Software Is for Sharing," published by *Time* magazine on July 30, 1984. If you can get access to it, you'll see that the article describes the problem of splitting software from the physical electronic platform for which it was created. The reason I say "if you can get access" is that – delightfully! – this article about free availability is behind a paywall at the *Time* website.

There may be good reasons for that. *Time* is providing a service to make the article available, and the author may still want the copyright to be enforced. In many cases, people write stuff to get paid. But how is that kind of "stuff" different from the stuff piled up in garages and storage units? How can we make better use of all *that* kind of stuff, the kind that is made up of information?

The notion of "open source" is generally associated with software, but people in many fields have long recognized the underlying problem: information wants to be free.[9] "Free" might mean *libre*, or exempt from restrictions – no restrictions on publication or dissemination. But "free" also has the literal meaning of *gratis*, being available without charge, and available for adaptation to different uses.[10] One advantage of an "open source" resource is that it connects with Thierer's (2014) "permissionless innovation," by letting people who have a problem adapt something devised for use in another setting.[11] The development of "society" is a process, and reductions in transaction costs on every dimension accelerate that process by allowing many basic routines and processes to be used as if they were available in the library.

Open source software is freely available, freely reproducible, freely editable, and technology neutral.[12] Note that that doesn't mean

---

[9] This phrase, or the sentiment it embodies, is ancient, as Clarke (1999) shows. But the modern use in the context of software and widely disseminated information is usually dated to 1984 and a conversation between Stewart Brand and Steve Wozniak:

> BRAND: It seems like there's a couple of interesting paradoxes that we're working here. ... On the one hand information wants to be expensive, because it's so valuable. The right information in the right place just changes your life. On the other hand, information wants to be free, because the cost of getting it out is getting lower and lower all the time. So you have these two fighting against each other.
>   WOZNIAK: Information should be free but your time should not.
>   BRAND: But then, at what point of amplification is your time being so well rewarded that it's getting strange or so under-rewarded that it's strange? There's problems there with the market.

Quoted in Brand and Herron (1985).

[10] See Clarke (1999) for more on the distinction.

[11] Hume (2004) saw the problem clearly:

> To form society, 'tis requisite not only that it be advantageous, but also that men be sensible of these advantages; and 'tis impossible, in their wild uncultivated state, that by study and reflexion alone, they should ever be able to attain this knowledge.

We can't know what innovations will be useful, either in their first or in their subsequent forms. The argument for experimentation and trial-and-error innovation, with the kind of reduced transaction costs that include open source information, is precisely that we cannot foresee what will be useful "by study and reflexion alone."

[12] The full requirements to qualify as "open source" are more extensive, and more technical. See Open Source Initiative (n.d.). Importantly, however, the protocol clearly includes source code, not just compiled programs.

all "free" software is open source; free software can be purchased at a zero price, but you may not be able to edit and adapt, or even view, the source code. An example of open source software is the Linux operating system, which some argue (because it is constantly adapted by almost everyone) is more stable and secure than proprietary systems. Interestingly, the Bitcoin software, which operates as a distributed system to manage the Bitcoin internet currency, is open source and can be copied and edited by anyone. Wikipedia, the "free" online encyclopedia, can be edited, pretty much in its entirety, by anyone. Of course, no one else is obliged to use your version of Bitcoin software, or your version of the Battle of Waterloo on Wikipedia. But you are free to use it.

Making useful things freely available obviously has some advantages. But it also creates a problem. Society needs inventors to discover new information, programmers to create new software, and researchers to learn more about the Battle of Waterloo. We have to cover the average costs of these valuable services somehow.

But once that new information is discovered, and once that software is written, at that point the information "wants" to be priced at marginal cost. In the case of data, source code, or ideas, this notion of price is difficult to sustain. The cost of dissemination is a few keystrokes, an internet connection, and space to store the digital content. Information needs to be *libre*, but it can't be *gratis*. How can we manage that? How can societies share what we already have, but also induce individuals to make more? The answer will require entrepreneurs.

THE MIDDLEMAN: A WORD ON ENTREPRENEURS

A "real" entrepreneur does not (just) take advantage of errors (i.e., differences) in prices or act as a go-between to move stuff that's in the wrong place. An entrepreneur imagines new products, or new ways of making the products. The "middleman" connects buyers and sellers and delivers the products. That may not be an accurate distinction, but it is a common one in the public mind. We tend to admire entrepreneurs, but we look down on intermediaries.

Entrepreneurs just seem more creative, more "aware" or "alert" – Israel Kirzner's terms – to new possibilities, sometimes even imagining products and innovations that consumers don't even want because they don't know they are possible.[13] Steve Jobs, of Apple Computer, famously observed that entrepreneurs could not rely on academic notions of "market demand." Jobs said, "You can't just ask customers what they want and then try to give that to them. By the time you get it built, they'll want something new" (Burlington, 1989).

This kind of "entrepreneurship as imagination" is crucially linked to the changes in the forms and availability of information. The distinction between middlemen and entrepreneurs is rapidly blurring because improvements in the "middleman" function – connecting buyers and sellers – are among the most fertile new spaces for entrepreneurial reimaginings.

That's not an easy thing to get your head around. If anything, "eliminate the middleman" is the maxim of many simplistic schemes for increasing profit or reducing costs. An example may help: suppose that Arthur owns a Sonic Screwdriver (if you aren't a Dr. Who fan, just accept that it's a useful thing), and is willing to rent it out for any price over $40 per day. Barbara wants to use a Sonic Screwdriver for a day and will pay any price less than $75. In principle, there is room for a deal because any rental offer greater than $40 and less than $75 makes both parties better off. And in a social sense the Sonic Screwdriver "should" be used by Barbara

---

[13] As Kirzner (1971) put it:

> The technical availability of profitable capital-using methods of production and of savings to provide the necessary capital, is not sufficient to ensure that these methods will be undertaken. *They constitute an opportunity for intertemporal exchange which may never be exploited if no one is aware of it.* If, at any time, such an opportunity remains as yet unexploited, it offers opportunity for entrepreneurial profit. An entrepreneur will be able to borrow capital, buy resources, and produce output at a market value that will more than repay the capitalist's investment together with the interest necessary to persuade him to advance the capital funds. (emphasis added)

because it creates more value (at least $75) in her hands than it does in Arthur's (no more than $40).

But Arthur may not know where or even who Barbara is, and it's expensive to go looking. They may be physically distant, meaning that there are transport costs. The medium of exchange may be cumbersome, requiring costs to clear the transaction if it takes place. And they don't trust each other; the Sonic Screwdriver may be fragile, and Arthur worries Barbara might break it. These transaction costs could easily be $50 or more. It doesn't matter how the costs are split, but assume that transaction costs are split evenly, $25 each. That means that Arthur will require a payment of at least $65 to rent out the Sonic Screwdriver, and Barbara will pay at most $50. There is now no price where the transaction can take place. And because of this Arthur and Barbara may not even imagine the idea of renting Sonic Screwdriver. No one has ever tried to set up a Sonic Screwdriver rental company, and no entrepreneur has worked on developing institutions that would allow the selling of reduced transaction costs. The people who own Sonic Screwdrivers keep them in special locked containers, which themselves are expensive and bulky. No market there. No one can imagine renting the things.

Suppose, to be more practical, that instead of a Sonic Screwdriver we are talking about a car. It is tempting to think that the reason that Uber has succeeded is that it avoids the costs of complying with the regulations, taxes, and restrictions that affect taxis. And that may be part of the story. But if you call an Uber driver, they appear almost immediately; you don't have to wait, or wave at taxis that don't stop. The GPS software knows where you are. Further, you can see the name and license information of the driver, and you know the company has the driver's personal and financial information. You don't need to give the driver directions because the software takes care of that while you sit in the car and think about something else. And the driver is paid, and tipped, without you having to touch your wallet. Finally, *you* rate the driver and the ride, outsourcing trust for free to other riders but helping Uber provide better service. Drivers with an average rating, over the most recent 500 rides, less than the local average "acceptable" rating – determined by Uber – lose access to the Uber software (Uber, n.d.). In effect, they are fired, though they can apply for reinstatement after taking a "quality improvement course."

In short, Uber connects two people who already wanted to find each other, if they had known it. The difference between this and the Sonic Screwdriver example is that you and the driver know you are looking for each other because Uber has created a market. Uber is selling *brokerage* services, making it possible for that driver to find that rider. Uber makes money not by selling taxi services – the driver sells those – but by selling reductions in triangulation costs, transfer costs, and trust costs. Uber is a pure intermediary.[14] The key factor is the *entrepreneurial* innovation in software platforms that drives triangulation, transfer, and trust costs down to the point where that activity is profitable for the entrepreneur and – for the first time – mutually beneficial to the seller and the consumer.

THE POWER DRILL AGAIN: IT'S ABOUT TIME

I started out with an example: suppose I need to drill some holes in some furniture. There are at least 80 million power drills in closets and garages and sheds around the US. Many of these have been used for only a few minutes, and the average lifetime use of half of these power drills is less than 30 minutes, *total* (Friedman, 2013). It seems wasteful to have such replication and excess capacity since relatively few of these tools are being used at any particular moment. Others

---

[14] It is legitimate to point out that, as a "middleman," Uber may validate the preferences and biases of its customers, even if those preferences are not ethically defensible. A recent study (Ge et al., 2016) of ride-hailing service data shows that people with African American "sounding" names are much more likely to have rides cancelled, either as drivers (passengers cancel on seeing the name of the driver) or passengers (driver cancels on seeing the name of the passenger). Once could object that the same phenomenon is common in taxis (for example, Ayres, Vars, & Zakariya, 2006), with the difference being that the choice is based on the racial appearance of the passenger (or driver) or the neighborhood where the taxi is being sent. But the fact remains that Uber and Lyft are conduits for the preferences, ethically defensible or not, of the people being matched.

(Asdfasdfasd, 2013) have raised some valid objections, focusing on the transaction cost of avoiding the "waste" and pointing out (rightly) that if it were really possible, and desirable, to rent rather than own people would already be doing it. So, with existing ways of doing business, the "business opportunity" presented by the fact that everyone owns a drill but rarely uses it is not real. Fair enough.

But the "rent vs. own" distinction *with existing ways of doing business* misses the key distinction. What entrepreneurs do is change the way we do business. Just as Steve Jobs saw a new product, the entrepreneurs of the new economy are reimagining the way that we find, negotiate, pay, and rely on each other. If those three problems – triangulation, transaction, and trust – can be solved, then the problem of what we are exchanging becomes less important.

What we actually seek from a transaction involving an item such as a power drill is not exactly ownership of the thing called the tool but rather access to the services that the tool can provide. This sounds like some arcane distinction from *The Matrix* (1999), but the difference is essential.[15]

I don't need a drill. What I need is a hole in this wall, now, right here.

The question is how I can get that done reliably at the lowest total cost, including (crucially) transaction costs. What is required is the *services* – in effect, the time – of a drill and the (small) effort required to press the drill into the wallboard. Everything else is transaction costs, costs paid so that the *useful* time can be used productively.[16]

We need a more fundamental conception of what "transactions" really are. All we really want to buy is "a hole in this wall, right here" at (future) times at our (unpredictable) discretion. When we buy a commodity, particularly a "durable" commodity such as a

---

[15] [In the subway station] Neo: "Love is ... a *human* emotion." Rama-Kandra: "No, it's a word." Lana Wachowski and Lilly Wachowski, dirs., *Matrix Revolutions* (2003).

[16] As we will discuss later, all costs are transaction costs, from the perspective of the consumer. But a better definition for analytical purposes is the difference between production costs to the maker and total cost to the consumer.

power drill, what is being bought is the ability to make a hole in any wall, anytime, conveniently. We own the drill because that guarantees immediate access because we are not sure when we'll need it.

That "when" suggests that what is missing from the discussion of the power drill, and the rent vs. own choice, is the idea of time.[17] If I buy something, I own it. But then I *still* rent it; I just "rent" it from myself. The point is that it is the *services* of the thing, over time, that I want. This aspect of time is only true for durable products, of course. If I buy an apple, and eat it, it's gone. But if I buy a drill, or a business suit, it's the stream of services that I expect to rent from the owner (even if that owner happens to be me) that motivates the transaction. When I want to use the drill, I have to walk out to the garage, find it amid all the other tools on the bench, and then walk back into the house, or wherever I want to make holes or drive screws.

Here's the thing: those who have objected (rightly) that it is not economic to rent a power drill are missing the point. It's not *intrinsically* more expensive to rent; there is no Eleventh Commandment that says: "Thou shalt not rent; rather, thou shalt own all things that are meet for all purposes, all the days of thy life." The choice depends on *institutions*.[18] By creating software platforms, entrepreneurs can produce – and

[17] As Rizzo (1996, p. 2) put it:

> To say that Austrian economics is the economics of time and ignorance is to say that it is the economics of coping with the problems posed by real time and radical ignorance.
>
> Although individuals are not paralyzed by these problems, they do not automatically or completely overcome them. *The behavior generated by this predicament in which human beings find themselves is a source of market phenomena and institutions.* It is also the source of prudential limits to these institutions. Human beings are "prisoners of time." (quoted from Shackle, 1970, p. 21). In the Austrian view, this prison acts not only as a constraint (i.e., the allocational aspects of time) but also as a formulator of experience, thus generating and limiting our knowledge." (emphasis added)

[18] "These individual actions are really trans-actions instead of either individual behavior or the "exchange" of commodities. It is this shift from commodities and individuals to transactions and working rules of collective action that marks the transition from the classical and hedonic schools to the institutional schools of economic thinking. The shift is a change in the ultimate unit of economic investigation. The classic and hedonic economists, with their communistic and

sell! – reductions in the costs of renting. That sounds awkward because we are not used to thinking about "producing reductions." But you had better get used to thinking that way. My prediction about this process is usefully separated into three parts:

(1) The third great economic revolution will be based on innovations that focus on digital tools that reduce transaction costs, *not* on the creation of new physical products themselves.

(2) The result will be that society will be able to make much more intensive use of durables of all kinds, as "excess capacity" becomes a *commodity to be sold* instead of a storage problem. The result will be that the quality and durability of the items being rented will increase sharply, but also that the quantity of items actually in circulation will plummet.

(3) People will collect experiences, not belongings, and the idea of ownership will seem quaint and archaic by the end of this century. Very few people under the age of thirty will have driver's licenses. Or jobs.

In the next chapter, I consider the problem of economic revolution and the destructive power of evolving institutions.

anarchistic offshoots, founded their theories on the relation of man to nature, but institutionalism is a relation of man to man. The smallest unit of the classic economists was a commodity produced by labor. The smallest unit of the hedonic economists was the same or similar commodity enjoyed by ultimate consumers. One was the objective side, the other the subjective side, of the same relation between the individual and the forces of nature. The outcome, in either case, was the materialistic metaphor of an automatic equilibrium, analogous to the waves of the ocean, but personified as "seeking their level." But the smallest unit of the institutional economists is a unit of activity – a transaction, with its participants. Transactions intervene between the labor of the classic economists and the pleasures of the hedonic economists, simply because it is society that controls access to the forces of nature, and transactions are, not the "exchange of commodities," but the alienation and acquisition, between individuals, of the rights of property and liberty created by society, which must therefore be negotiated between the parties concerned before labor can produce, or consumers can consume, or commodities be physically exchanged." (Commons, 1931, pp. 653–654).

2   Division of Labor, Destruction, and Revolution

Man experiences a multitude of needs, on whose satisfaction his happiness depends, and whose non-satisfaction entails suffering. Alone and isolated, he could only provide in an incomplete, insufficient manner for these incessant needs. The instinct of sociability brings him together with similar persons, and drives him into communication with them. Therefore, impelled by the self-interest of the individuals thus brought together, a certain division of labor is established, necessarily followed by exchanges. In brief, we see an organization emerge, by means of which man can more completely satisfy his needs than he could living in isolation.

... This natural organization is called society. The object of society is therefore the most complete satisfaction of man's needs. The division of labor and exchange are the means by which this is accomplished.

Molinari, 1849, pp. 17–18

The big difference between an economy based on selling stuff and an economy focused on selling reductions in transaction costs is that we can make better use of things we already own. But the effects of this transformation from selling to sharing, like the results of the first two revolutions – the Neolithic and the Industrial – may be disruptive. Some of the institutions we have come to depend on will be swept away, and attempts to preserve the approaches we have long depended on are likely to cause unnecessary and very costly delays because it's hard to foresee just how the new system will work.

The Neolithic Revolution made it possible for humans to enter complex relations of more or less voluntary dependence and to share economies of organization and information. The Industrial Revolution created an astonishing burst of productivity, which made ownership of a bewildering variety of commodities and tools possible for all but the poorest of people, where just fifty years before such items would have been denied of all but the wealthiest.

In this chapter, I will first describe why exchange and sharing are so important for the flourishing of human beings. Then I'll describe briefly how the first two great economic revolutions came about, and how each used cooperation through division of labor to make human thriving possible.

EXCHANGE AND SHARING AS COOPERATION

Voluntary exchange is amazing. Gifts are nice, but no one can depend on gifts as a permanent source of nutrition or protection, and in any case gifts are essentially unknown outside of human societies. In the animal kingdom, and for that matter in the plant kingdom, too, self-interest dominates action and choice through evolution and natural selection of genes that conform to selfishness.[1]

Human societies are mutually dependent, but with cooperation, in the sense that people specialize and then rely on others to provide the goods and services they don't make themselves. These dependency relations can be exploitative, of course, as when one people or group enslaves another and steals what it produces. But human dependency in most societies is cooperative. As I said earlier, Adam Smith's basic human tendency to "truck, barter, and exchange" is based on an even deeper cooperative impulse. A number of scholars have written about this impulse, which appears consistent with a behavioral bias toward cooperation.

---

[1] There are many examples of actions that look like "gifts," such as the nectar flowers give to bees or other pollinators, or the nutritious "packets" that encase sperm in a variety of insects. But the nectar is clearly an inducement, or implicitly an exchange in compensation for pollination services. As for insects, consider the "gift" in context:

In crickets and katydids, it is not uncommon for the male to vibrate his body at this point, a behavior known as "tremulation," which helps the female orient herself for mating. The male not only offers the female a sperm packet (spermatophore), but he also may offer her a "nutritional gift" intended for consumption during mating. In mating Broad-winged Tree Crickets, the female will climbed [sic] on top of the male (this is the case for most crickets) and will be feeding on secretions from glands on his back, as he prepares to transfer a spermatophore from the tip of his tail to her tail.

(*"Song of Insects,"* 2017)

If instead of "nutritional gift" one said "box of chocolates" this all sounds pretty familiar. But it's not *really* a gift, is it?

Gerald Gaus makes the claim in *The Order of Public Reason* (2010, p. 96) that humans are "rule-following conditional cooperators." Social scientists have come to realize that cooperation is *intrinsically* valued, and noncooperation punished, by groups of humans. Thus, there are really two problems:

(1) Do humans obey rules, or break rules, as a matter of their own preference (that is, do people *like* following rules, separate from other material benefits we receive as a consequence of following rules)?
(2) Are humans evolved to have an emotional, non-reasoned reaction of anger when someone else is seen to *break* the rules?

If the answer to the first question is "yes," we expect that most people will obey the rules unless there are strong material reasons not to. If the answer to the second question is "yes," then the public good of norm enforcement will be supplied by people, almost against their will. If you see someone break the rules, you will think, "I shouldn't say anything," but your body will be suffused with a cocktail of chemicals that are likely to lead to a confrontation.

There is no question that the biology of cooperation and detection of defection is deeply embedded in our mental architecture as a behavioral inheritance. The biologist E. O. Wilson put it this way, in his book *The Meaning of Human Existence*:

> The competition between [selfishness and altruism] can be succinctly expressed as follows: Within groups selfish individuals beat altruistic individuals, but groups of altruists beat groups of selfish individuals. Or, risking oversimplification, individual selection promoted sin, while group selection promoted virtue.
>
> *(Wilson, p. 33)*

What economists have discovered is that voluntary exchange is one of the most important form of cooperation in human societies.[2]

---

[2] Some scholars have gone even further, claiming that cooperation and "mutual aid" is the basis of almost all relationships in nature. The famed bio-anarchist Piotr Kropotkin (1902, p. 14) claimed that the behavioral advantages of cooperation, or

Consider the story of R. A. Radford, a British economist who was captured during WWII and sent to a German POW camp.

> Very soon after capture people realised that it was both undesirable and unnecessary, in view of the limited size and the equality of supplies, to give away or to accept gifts of cigarettes or food. "Goodwill" developed into trading as a more equitable means of maximising individual satisfaction.
>
>   We reached a transit camp in Italy about a fortnight after capture and received ¼ of a Red Cross food parcel each a week later. At once exchanges, already established, multiplied in volume. Starting with simple direct barter, such as a non-smoker giving a smoker friend his cigarette issue in exchange for a chocolate ration, more complex exchanges soon became an accepted custom.
>
> *(Radford, 1945, pp. 190–191)*

Radford was not saying gifts were wrong. Rather, people find ways to "truck, barter, and exchange" that make both parties to the exchange better off. As we will see later in this chapter, this requires an ability to conceive of an abstraction: For me to understand how to make you better off, I have to be able to put myself in your place. And that is just what I am doing when I offer a voluntary exchange: I have to offer something you actually want.[3]

what he called "mutual aid," were so great that the state would eventually become unnecessary. The reason was that people would come to accept that cooperation was always better, even though cheating might have been momentarily advantageous.

A soon as we study animals ... we at once perceive that though there is an immense amount of warfare and extermination going on amidst various species. ... There is, at the same time, as much, or perhaps even more, of mutual support, mutual aid, and mutual defense amidst animals belonging to the same species or, at least, to the same society. Sociability is as much a law of nature as mutual struggle ... [Cooperation] favors the development of such habits and characters as insure the maintenance and further development of the species, together with the greatest amount of welfare and enjoyment of life for the individual, with the least waste of energy.

(Kropotkin, 1902, Chapter 1)

[3] The definition of "voluntary" may be problematic. One way of approaching the problem is to identify conditions under which an exchange is truly voluntary, or *euvoluntary*, in the phrase coined by Munger (2011).

THE ECONOMIC LOGIC OF SHARING

Until now, economic growth has been caused by the expansion of opportunities for entrepreneurs and producers to imagine things that consumers want. A trader who travels to the Spice Islands of the South Pacific is trying to figure out which spices to buy, based not on what he wants but on what he thinks consumers will want back in Venice or Paris. An inventor is trying to imagine new ways of organizing durable capital equipment so that products can be made at lower cost and with greater quality. An entrepreneur is trying to imagine new products, things no one has ever seen, but which they will want right away when they do see it.

The third economic revolution will be different. *Sharing* is one of the central concepts in this book because it is at the center of Tomorrow 3.0. To see why sharing is so important, I want to quote a passage from Matt Ridley's book, *The Rational Optimist* (2011). Ridley is not the first to say some of these things, but the way he puts things together here is marvelous.

> The Sun King [Louis XIV, King of France from 1643 to 1715] had dinner each night alone. He chose from forty dishes, served on gold and silver plate. It took a staggering 498 people to prepare each meal ... At that time, the average French family would have prepared and consumed its own meals as well as paid tax to support his servants in the palace. So it is not hard to conclude that Louis XIV was rich *because* others were poor. (Ridley, pp. 36–37)
>
> But what about today? Consider that you are an average person, say a thirty-five-year-old woman, living in, for the sake of argument, Paris, and earning the median wage, with a working husband and two children. You are far from poor, but in relative terms, you are immeasurably poorer than Louis XIV was. Where he was the richest of the rich in the world's richest city, you have no servants, no palace, no carriage, no kingdom. And yet, consider this: The cornucopia that greets you as you enter the supermarket dwarfs anything that Louis XIV ever experienced (and it is probably

less likely to contain salmonella). You can buy a fresh, frozen, tinned, smoked or pre-prepared meal made with beef, chicken, pork, lamb, fish, shrimp, scallops, eggs, potatoes, beans, carrots, cabbage, eggplants, kumquats, celeriac, okra, or seven kinds of lettuce, cooked in olive, walnut, sunflower, or peanut oil and flavored with cilantro, turmeric, basil, or rosemary.

You may have no chefs, but you can decide on a whim to choose between scores of nearby bistros or Italian, Chinese, Japanese, and Indian restaurants, in each of which a team of skilled chefs is waiting to serve your family at less than an hour's notice. Think of this: Never before this generation has the average person been able to afford to have somebody else prepare their meals.

You employ no tailor, but you can browse the Internet and instantly order from an almost infinite range of excellent, affordable clothes made of cotton, silk, linen, wool, or nylon in your size from factories all over Asia. You have no carriage, but you can buy a ticket which will summon the services of a skilled pilot of a budget airline to fly you to one of hundreds of destinations that Louis XIV never dreamed of seeing. You have no woodcutters to bring you logs for the fire, but the operators of gas rigs in Russia are clamoring to bring you clean central heating. You have no private apothecary, but your local pharmacy supplies you with the handiwork of many thousands of chemists, engineers, and logistics experts. You have no government ministers, but diligent reporters are even now standing ready to tell you about a film star's divorce if you will only switch to their channel or log on to their blogs.

My point is that *you* have many more than Louis XIV's 498 servants at your immediate beck and call. Of course, unlike the Sun King's servants, these people work for many other people too, but from your perspective, what is the difference? That is the magic that exchange and specialization have wrought for the human species.

(Ridley, 2011, pp. 36–37)

Here are the three key insights of Ridley's simple but systematic summary.

(1) Specialization is a kind of sharing because we are dependent on each other. But rather than owning an entire person, or whole factory, we (in effect) share just the amount of specialized knowledge or service that we need. Some distant person on a production line works for 1.7 seconds on my new shoes, at a very low cost, and then 1.7 seconds on your shoes, and so on. We all share that person's knowledge, and the factory's equipment, very cheaply.

(2) The very fact that there is a factory reflects a particular kind of specialization called "division of labor." This specialized sharing produces Ridley's "cornucopia," a gigantic increase in the amount, and the variety, of products available to us.

(3) Clearly, specialization *can* be achieved in a "command," or government-organized, hierarchy. But the full benefits of sharing can only be realized in an exchange setting. The reason, as will be discussed later, is that the price signals are crucial for allocating resources, and profit signals are crucial for determining which new products should survive and which should be discarded. In command hierarchies, there is no effective way of determining when the commands are wrong, because people just do what they are told.

We have introduced the idea of voluntary exchange and shown why it amounts to a kind of sharing through specialization and the division of labor. Let's look back to see why these concepts are important by looking at the first two great economic revolutions.

THE FIRST GREAT ECONOMIC REVOLUTION: THE NEOLITHIC

In a period now known as the Holocene Epoch, several useful plants and a few animal species were domesticated.[4] This may have partly caused, and partly been caused by, a simultaneous move from nomadic hunting and gathering to relatively settled agriculture.

---

[4] In fact, Harari (2015, p. 80) argued that in some ways wheat domesticated humans, rather than the other way around:

The act of planting a field, fencing in some livestock, and then building a substantial hut and staying there may have seemed pretty trivial, but it changed everything.

Of course, looking back from the twenty-first century we call it the Holocene Epoch and think it was transformative. But the people living then just called it "Now." Why did they change the way they lived, after tens of thousands of years of nomadic roaming in small bands? Why did they convert to such a completely different way of living, starting to clear fields and construct fixed dwellings and fortifications? The change was wrenching, and revolutionary. Why do it? Why go along?

> Think for a moment about the Agricultural Revolution from the viewpoint of wheat. Ten thousand years ago wheat was just a wild grass, one of many, confined to a small range in the Middle East. Suddenly, within just a few short millennia, it was growing all over the world. According to the basic evolutionary criteria of survival and reproduction, wheat has become one of the most successful plants in the history of the earth. In areas such as the Great Plains of North America, where not a single wheat stalk grew 10,000 years ago, you can today walk for hundreds upon hundreds of miles without encountering any other plant. Worldwide, wheat covers about 870,000 square miles of the globe's surface, almost ten times the size of Britain. How did this grass turn from insignificant to ubiquitous?
>
> Wheat did it by manipulating Homo sapiens to its advantage. This ape had been living a fairly comfortable life hunting and gathering until about 10,000 years ago, but then began to invest more and more effort in cultivating wheat. Within a couple of millennia, humans in many parts of the world were doing little from dawn to dusk other than taking care of wheat plants. It wasn't easy. Wheat demanded a lot of them. Wheat didn't like rocks and pebbles, so Sapiens broke their backs clearing fields. Wheat didn't like sharing its space, water and nutrients with other plants, so men and women laboured long days weeding under the scorching sun. Wheat got sick, so Sapiens had to keep a watch out for worms and blight. Wheat was attacked by rabbits and locust swarms, so the farmers built fences and stood guard over the fields. Wheat was thirsty, so humans dug irrigation canals or lugged heavy buckets from the well to water it. Sapiens even collected animal faeces to nourish the ground in which wheat grew.
>
> The body of Homo sapiens had not evolved for such tasks. It was adapted to climbing apple trees and running after gazelles, not to clearing rocks and carrying water buckets. Human spines, knees, necks and arches paid the price. Studies of ancient skeletons indicate that the transition to agriculture brought about a plethora of ailments, such as slipped discs, arthritis and hernias. Moreover, the new agricultural tasks demanded so much time that people were forced to settle permanently next to their wheat fields. This completely changed their way of life. We did not domesticate wheat. It domesticated us. The word "domesticate" comes from the Latin domus, which means "house." Who's the one living in a house? Not the wheat. It's the Sapiens.

There have been groups of people for as long as there have been people. When humankind was still in the hunter-gatherer stage of its development, though, these groups consisted of no more than a family or perhaps a clan of several related families – such a group might range from 50 to 150 people, at the largest.[5] With constrained opportunities to specialize and limited economies of scale in military organization, there was little benefit to be derived from larger groups. Conflict between groups was frequent, but not – by modern standards – large scale, and was not particularly violent (Fry and Söderberg, 2013). This had nothing to do with the nobility of these savages but resulted from their universal poverty: Why fight if there is nothing worth taking?[6]

The move to fixed agriculture exposed people to violence because they were dependent on whomever was specializing in defending their crops, at least until they were harvested. Jared Diamond called the

---

[5] There is considerable controversy about the probable average, and variance, of the size of human bands in early hunter-gatherer settings. One famous benchmark is "Dunbar's Number," an estimate of stable group size of 100–230 people arrived at by Robin Dunbar (1992) using calculations based on the complexity of relations and the capacity of the human cortex to negotiate that complexity. However, this number is taken by anthropologists as an upper limit, including ancestral relations. A more accurate estimate for a stable group size is roughly fifty people, according to Dunbar's calculations. There have been interesting attempts to test, or perhaps validate, these limits on stable group size using data on Twitter "followers" (Gonçalves et al., 2011) and clans in the game World of Warcraft (Ducheneaut, Nicholas & Nicholas Yee, 2009). In a quite different setting, and through what appears to be pure trial and error, Hutterite settlements have a division rule settled on more than a century ago. When the group reaches a size of 125–150 people, the group divides in half and forms two new colonies (Ryan, 1977). This rule appears to optimize both on the maximum size, where it becomes too difficult to run the colony communally, and on the minimum side, where 60–75 people are required to establish a successful communal colony. This same theme is developed in more theoretical terms in Gladwell (2000).

[6] One must be careful lest a note of the "noble savage" kind of thinking creep into our conception of hunter-gatherer tribes. While many scholars would still claim that conflict among tribes is likely to involve threat displays and counting "coup" more often than actual violence, Lawrence Keeley (1997) argued that some tribes in close proximity might be at war 60 percent of the time, or more. Further, Keeley claims that casualty rates among adult males might be in excess of 50 percent in some encounters. While others have disputed these numbers, hard data on pre-historic societies are by their nature hard to obtain. On violence in traditional human societies and the transition to settled agriculture, see Barker (2009), Braidwood (1960), and Diamond (2013).

move to fixed agriculture "The worst mistake in the history of the human race" (1987, p. 64) and he was not entirely kidding.[7] This seems surprising. If the Neolithic Revolution was so bad, then (1) why did people accept the change, and (2) why didn't evolutionary forces select for the superior way of living, causing nomads to out-compete farmers?

The answer is that that is the wrong way to think about economic revolutions. It's true that the quality of life, *for individuals*, saw a net decline: People had shorter lives, smaller physical stature, and skeletal robustness as well as less varied and nutritious diets. They also suffered from communicable diseases caught by staying in one place as well as living near domesticated animals and their own human feces. On the economic side, things were also worse. For the first time, people had "jobs," and they worked much longer hours, with more repetition and less control over how they spent their time. Nobody would have made that switch voluntarily.

The problem is that treating the switch from nomadic hunter-gatherer to fixed agriculture as a voluntary *choice* is misleading. Institutions, or systems of organizing society, were calling the shots. Within just a few thousand years, the new system of fixed agriculture allowed societies that used it to become more powerful, economically and voluntarily. Fixed agriculture fostered something called specialization. Specialization seems innocuous, but it is a transformative and corrosive force.

---

[7] Yuval Harari goes further, calling the switch from nomadic to agricultural life "history's biggest fraud."

> Rather than heralding a new era of easy living, the Agricultural Revolution left farmers with lives generally more difficult and less satisfying than those of foragers. Hunter-gatherers spent their time in more stimulating and varied ways, and were less in danger of starvation and disease. The Agricultural Revolution certainly enlarged the sum total of food at the disposal of humankind, but the extra food did not translate into a better diet or more leisure. Rather, it translated into population explosions and pampered elites. The average farmer worked harder than the average forager, and got a worse diet in return. The Agricultural Revolution was history's biggest fraud.

(Harari, 2015, p. 79)

Specialization is limited by the extent of the cooperation horizon, which in most cases is the "size" of the group that is cooperating.[8] But specialization also *determines* the extent of the cooperation horizon. The reason the Neolithic Revolution was irresistible was that it made possible something brand-new: cities. And cities could support armies, overwhelming the ability of any but the most isolated tribes to choose any other form of society.[9]

The move to fixed agriculture, and then to cities, at first caused a net *reduction* in the quality of life for each person, compared to the *average* person before the change. But the *total number* of people grew at least 100 times as large, within just a few generations, and continued to expand dramatically for the next 1,000 years.[10]

Not by accident, there was also an explosion in the development of military tactics and equipment. Agriculture required that people stay in one place to reap what they had sown. The accumulation of surpluses from one season to the next was the first step toward civilization, but it also meant that people now had wealth–crops, herds of animals, and tools–*worth* stealing.[11] Once "property" was

---

[8] In Adam Smith's terms, "division of labor is limited by the extent of the market" (1981, p. 31).

[9] This claim is not literally true. As Hummel (2001) argued, some sense of national identity or unifying ideology could unite disparate groups. And as Scott (2010) points out, some groups will go to great lengths not to be governed. But barring a special ideological or geographic feature, the vast majority of instances (Laet, 1994, pp. 372–373) seem to support the claim that cities, and later states, win.

[10] The story is more complicated than this, in terms of the expansion of human population. As Aiméa et al. (2013) have found, the increase in population often attributed to the development of fixed agriculture and the Neolithic actually occurred much earlier, in the Paleolithic, perhaps as much as 60,000 years ago. But even in this case it is likely that the move to fixed agriculture was the result of population pressure, and in turn specialization then enabled the development of cities.

[11] David Friedman (2000, pp. 118–119) offers a half-serious explanation for the emergence of "civilization": dogs. He claims that dogs reduced the transaction cost of private property by making it possible to enforce territories of exclusive use. The solution was efficient before that, in the sense that a binding agreement would have made everyone better off. But the resources required to enforce property rights in scattered, poorly organized groups would have consumed more than all the gains from the increased efficiency of a property rights system. Domesticating dogs dramatically reduced the transaction costs of maintaining a system of territorial

established as a convention, neighboring farmers realized that instead of stealing from each other – and thus forcing one another to waste time defending their crops – they *could* both be better off if they cooperated. And since there are important economies of scale in defense, if many farmers could band together, build walls, and develop better weapons they could protect each farmer's wealth much more efficiently.[12]

But the raiders also had a problem: If they stole too much, too often, the farmers would die, and there would be nothing left to steal. Further, if the farmers knew they were going to be robbed, they would not plant crops or keep animals, and again there would be nothing to steal.[13] Perhaps some of the farmers decided to specialize, exchanging the digging sticks of farmers for the spears of warriors. Of course, that meant they couldn't grow food anymore, so military specialists became dependent on the community for food, just as the farmers were dependent on military specialists.

Societies came to be organized as groups of farmers ruled and protected by what Mancur Olson (1993, p. 568) calls "stationary

"property" because dogs are a genetic credible commitment. Their senses of smell and hearing are strong enough that ambush is impossible, and even trespassing is costly. And the dog, lacking reason, will certainly attack and try to bite intruders, even at risk to itself. The dog is not smart enough to be anything but brave. Friedman recognizes the story is perhaps too pat, so he closes by noting, "Si non è vero è ben trovato," or "If it isn't true, it should be."

[12] See, for details, North (1981). It is certainly possible that the group did not "realize" that stealing was a poor strategy – even for the thieves – in a setting of repeated interaction. The convention of property ownership and deference to ownership of others – including ownership and control by the state or monarch – is just one possible outcome. The claim is not that all societies made this jump, but rather that those societies that did make that jump tended to grow faster and become more militarily powerful.

[13] The stores of wealth created by settled agriculture, however, may also have invited theft by roving bandits (Olson, 1982; 2000; Olson and McGuire, 1996), which suggests a very different account of the origins of political authority. These bandits could steal in a day what the farmers had taken years to accumulate. Consequently, farmers had to expend resources to keep their holdings safe. These resources are a waste, however, because spending on defense produces no additional calories or useful products; it just protects the food and resources one has already produced. Having to pay for the defense of agriculture is a kind of transaction cost: You gain nothing from defense, but the failure to defend can cost you everything.

bandits."[14] This transformation happened in many places around the world as people began to settle down and develop societies that consisted of more than tiny clans. The existence of something like property rights internalized problems of theft and the communal use of resources.[15]

Consequently, the Neolithic Revolution – through sharing and specialization – allowed an enormous increase in human population and the concentration of groups of people in new, dense social arrangements called "cities." A city of 10,000 *requires*, but can also *support*, specialists. On one hand, people who specialize become much more knowledgeable and productive. But people also become dependent – and if they are highly specialized, *entirely* dependent – on others for providing the necessities of life. If I spend all my time making spear points or tanning leather, for example, I'll starve unless someone grows my food and I'll freeze unless someone brings me firewood.

This change, once it has begun, is both irresistible and irreversible. As a specialist becomes much more productive through practice, the creation of tools, the discovery of techniques made possible by experimentation based on a shorter production cycle, and the

---

[14] For other work on the stationary bandit, see Skaperdas (1992, 2001), Konrad (2009), and Kurrild-Klitgaard and Svendson (2003).

[15] It is possible that before this transformation the rights to use hunting territory and other primitive resources had been held in common without any special problems of inefficiency. The Lockean account of the origins of property rights rests on the perfectly sensible idea that combining labor with a widely available resource creates a right, though perhaps not a right that is formally defined or can be defended. It is more likely, however, as has been argued by Demsetz (1967), that property rights were an unnecessarily costly innovation as long as there was "as much and as good" of the resource. It is precisely the moment when scarcity begins to bite that organizing property rights pays off in terms of internalizing the external effects of inefficient overuse. In that case, the proximate cause of the development of property rights and the move from informal sharing arrangements was the increasing population. It was the consequent confrontation with scarcity that caused the move to fixed agriculture and property rights. As there were many more people on the same land, the inefficiencies of the "commons" (Hardin, 1968, p. 1243) meant that groups that failed to innovate either starved or were wiped out militarily, or else lost members to migration and secession. A version of this account is given by North, Wallis, & Weingast (2013).

ability to preserve and hand down new knowledge become part of the legacy of humankind. This accumulation of capital, including physical tools and – importantly – specific technical *knowledge* could be learned, remembered, and taught.

- The change was *irreversible* because specialization created so much more capital, and so many more people, that the old system could no longer support the new population.
- The reason the change is *irresistible* is that the economies of scale in military specialization are overwhelming. Hunter-gatherers couldn't survive separately and were overwhelmed.

There is one point I made above, almost in passing, to which we should now return. That is the complex but important relation between specialization and the size of the group. In particular, *the degree of specialization is limited by the extent of the cooperation horizon.* Let's see why this relation is so crucial to the story of economic revolutions, and why it is relevant for the world of Tomorrow 3.0.

Why Specialization Is Limited by the Cooperation Horizon

Within a thousand years after the development of fixed agriculture, cities grew up where there had been only small, temporary settlements. Cities, allowed – and in fact required – a high degree of organization and specialization to survive. Specialization caused an enormous increase in the output of tools, food, knowledge of materials science such as metallurgy, and the variety of products.

The beginnings of trade allowed even more specialization: Even if you couldn't make it, you could trade for it. Pressure was placed on military capacity to control trade routes, not just to defend walled cities, as a few large city-states sought to ensure access to sources of metals, minerals, and other natural resources. The cooperation horizon expanded from the walls of the city to the routes along which trade was possible. That meant that the larger the area – the size of the cooperation horizon – controlled by a ruler or kingdom, the greater the degree of specialization that was enabled.

Of course, this "specialization" was often *directed*, rather than emerging from any entrepreneurial impulse based on profit. Rulers and kings commissioned artisans as local monopolists, and guilds policed this monopoly through a system of master and apprentice, or master and slaves.[16] The degree of specialization this system could achieve was impressive, but it was largely artisanal rather than industrial. Each village would have a "charter" (from the king, who specialized in military force) for one artisan to specialize, developing skills as a shoemaker, brewer, crockery-maker, blacksmith, and so on. A primitive system of mutual dependence supported this specialization, and it benefited the king to be able to revoke a charter or withhold the enforcement of the monopoly that made specialization valuable.

Artisanal specialization is an important step: One skilled cobbler could make ten times as many shoes as an untrained person, with better quality, and a skilled cobbler could pass on the knowledge and tricks of the trade that had taken centuries to put together. But the technology is linear: Two cobblers, working with two sets of foot-molds and tools, could make only twice as many shoes as one cobbler. To serve increased populations, you had to keep adding cobblers. And there was no particular value in trading between villages because each had its own chartered cobbler. Each city was self-sufficient, with the degree of specialization governed by the size of the city.

Still, it was possible for even this relatively simple system of cooperation and mutual dependence to support far more people than small hunter-gatherer groups could support. As Plato put it:

> A State [arises] out of the needs of mankind; no one is self-sufficing, but all of us have many wants ... Then, as we have many wants, and many persons are needed to supply them, one takes a helper ... and

---

[16] In *The Theory of Economic History*, economist John Hicks details how this system, in surprisingly similar ways and with surprisingly few differences, worked in Europe, Japan, China, and the Middle East for 3,000 years. North, Wallis, and Weingast, in their book *Violence and Social Orders*, note that this system produces a stable, but unfortunate, feedback that locks in the closed and exclusive set of rights that limit sharing and exchange but which promote specialization.

another ... [W]hen these partners and helpers are gathered together
in one habitation the body of inhabitants is termed a State ...
And they exchange with one another, and one gives, and another
receives, under the idea that the exchange will be for their good.

(The Republic, Book II)

This idea of the city-state, or polis, as the nexus – but also the
limit – of cooperation, is a potent tool for the social theorist. It is easy
to see that the extent of specialization was limited by the size of the
cooperation horizon: A small, nomadic clan has one person who plays
on a hollow log with sticks; a moderately-sized town might have a
string quartet; and a city could support a symphony.

One of the earliest sociologists, Muslim scholar Ibn Khaldun
(1332–1406), described what he called "cooperation" as a means of
achieving the benefits of specialization:

The power of the individual human being is not sufficient for him
to obtain (the food) he needs, and does not provide him with as
much food as he requires to live. Even if we assume an absolute
minimum of food – that is, food enough for one day, (a little) wheat,
for instance – that amount of food could be obtained only after
much preparation such as grinding, kneading, and baking. Each of
these three operations requires utensils and tools that can be
provided only with the help of several crafts, such as the crafts of
the blacksmith, the carpenter, and the potter. Assuming that a man
could eat unprepared grain, an even greater number of operations
would be necessary in order to obtain the grain: sowing and reaping,
and threshing to separate it from the husks of the ear. Each of these
operations requires a number of tools and many more crafts than
those just mentioned. It is beyond the power of one man alone to
do all that, or (even) part of it, by himself. Thus, he cannot do
without a combination of many powers from among his fellow
beings, if he is to obtain food for himself and for them.
Through co-operation, the needs of a number of persons, many
times greater than their own (number), can be satisfied.

(Khaldun, 2015, p. 46)

Bernard Mandeville, in his *Fable of the Bees*, recognized that specialization might be mutually beneficial because of the consequent increase in total output enjoyed by all.

> [I]f one will wholly apply himself to the making of Bows and Arrows, whilst another provides Food, a third builds Huts, a fourth makes Garments, and a fifth Utensils, they not only become useful to one another, but the Callings and Employments themselves will in the same Number of Years receive much greater Improvements, than if all had been promiscuously followed by every one of the Five.
>
> *(Mandeville, 2016, p. 370)*

This interpretation of specialization, and what was later called "division of labor," has long been a central theme of sociology. Investments in specialization, arising as a consequence of direction, limited by the size of the city, later motivated scholars such as Emile Durkheim (1858–1917) to recognize the central importance of division of labor for the thriving of humankind. As Durkheim (1984, p. 17) put it, "the economic services that it can render are insignificant compared with the moral effect that it produces, and its true function is to create between two or more people a feeling of solidarity."

What that means is that specialization and the mutual dependence it fostered first enabled the construction of cities, and then made cities necessary. The interesting thing is that no one may have intended these developments, but on the other hand no one could resist them, either. The degree of specialization is limited by the extent of the cooperation horizon. Cities were the first institution that fostered an expanded cooperation horizon.

But another institution was on the horizon, an institution that forced a different kind of cooperation and dependence, and which destroyed many of the cultural and social arrangements that had relied on artisanal production. That new institution was markets, animating the industrial revolution in a drive for profits. And once again this second revolution, like the first, was a product of human nature and human action but not of human choice.[17]

THE SECOND REVOLUTION: PRODUCING
AND OWNING

The second great economic transformation was the Industrial Revolution, often dated back to the period between 1760 and 1850. The antecedents were visible before 1760, and the consequences were still playing out well after 1850, but this was the period of the most intensive upheaval. In the eighteenth century, a number of entrepreneurs, operating independently and without any central coordination, began to try production processes that differed sharply from the artisanal culture. They began to form enterprises ("entrepreneur" means "one who undertakes") that divided the production process among (at first) several, and (later) many, individual workers. It took far less time to master a single step in the production process, and the worker assigned that step was able to develop dexterity and specialized tools. The most famous example is Adam Smith's celebrated "pin factory," which Smith believed had eighteen main steps or operations, performed by different workers.[18]

---

[17] With an obvious debt to Adam Ferguson (1996, p. 119), who said: "Every step and every movement of the multitude, even in what are termed enlightened ages, are made with equal blindness to the future; and nations stumble upon establishments, which are indeed the result of human action, but not the execution of any human design."

[18] Smith had certainly read du Monceau on pins, who had said:

There is nobody who is not surprised of the small price of pins; but we shall be even more surprised, when we know how many different operations, most of them very delicate, are mandatory to make a good pin. We are going to go through these operations in a few words to stimulate the curiosity to know their detail; this enumeration will supply as many articles which will make the division of this work ... The first operation is to have brass go through the drawing plate to calibrate it.

(Monceau, 1761, p. 41)

Interestingly, there is speculation that Smith may have read "the division of this work" (Monceau's book) as "division of the work of pin-making." Or, not. It's just speculation.

Smith's Insight: Markets Substitute for Cities as Limits on the Cooperation Horizon

It is common to say that Adam Smith "invented" or "advocated" division of labor. Such claims are simply mistaken, on several grounds (see, for a discussion, Kennedy 2008). What Smith actually did was to describe in detail how decentralized market exchange promotes the division of labor *across* political units, rather than just *within* them as previous thinkers had discussed. Smith had two key insights:

First, the division of labor would be powerful even if all human beings were identical because many important differences in productive capacity are learned.[19] We don't have to have innate differences for markets to work. But if there are innate differences, markets can take advantage of that fact.

Second, the division of labor gives rise to *market* institutions and expands the extent of the market. Exchange relations relentlessly push against borders and expand the effective locus of cooperation. The benefit to the individual is that first dozens, then hundreds, and ultimately millions, of other people stand ready to "work for" each of us, in ways that are constantly being expanded into new activities and new products. Where division of labor had previously been limited by the size of the city, markets expanded the cooperation horizon dramatically, limited only by transaction costs. Once markets developed, there were powerful incentives for larger and larger groups to cooperate.[20]

---

[19] Smith's parable of the "street porter and the philosopher" illustrates the depth of this insight. As Smith put it:

[T]he very different genius which appears to distinguish men of different professions, when grown up to maturity, is not upon many occasions so much the *cause*, as the *effect* of the division of labour. The difference between the most dissimilar characters, between a philosopher and a common street porter, for example, seems to arise not so much from nature, as from habit, custom, and education.

(Smith, 1981, vol. 1, Ch 2; emphasis in original)

[20] Interestingly, this ability to make deals and cooperate may also operate in the area of producing "public goods." But as Cowen (1999) noted, this ability also allows for collusion and the creation of arrangements in restraint of trade. And as Adam Smith

Smith's example – the pin factory – has become one of the central tropes of economic theory. It is true that in the book Smith divides pin-making into eighteen operations, but that number is arbitrary: Labor is divided into the number of operations that fit the extent of the market. In a small market, perhaps three workers, each performing several different operations, could be employed. In a city or small country, as Smith saw, eighteen different workers might be employed. In an international market, the optimal number of workers (or their equivalent in automated steps) would be even larger.

The interesting point is that there would be constant pressure on the factory to do wo things

(a) expand the number of operations even more, and to automate them through the use of tools and other capital
(b) to expand the size of the market served. The consequence would be lower-cost pins because of expanded division of labor, but this in turn creates pressure to serve a larger market so that the expanded output could be sold.

Smith recognized this dynamic pressure in the form of what can only be regarded today as a theorem, the title of Chapter 3 in Book I of the *Wealth of Nations*: "That the Division of Labor is Limited by the Extent of the Market." George Stigler treated this claim as a testable theorem in his 1951 article and developed its insights in the context of modern economics. The size of the cooperation horizon, determined by politics, had evolved into the extent of the market, limited only by transaction costs.

The full importance of Smith's insight was not developed until quite recently. James Buchanan presented the starkest description of

said: "People of the same trade seldom meet together, even for merriment and diversion, but the conversation ends in a conspiracy against the public, or in some contrivance to raise prices." (Smith, 1981, p. 148). Smith's point was that it would difficult to suppress this impulse, but that it was unwise to reduce the transactions costs of such arrangements by reducing the transaction costs of such meeting. What Smith had in mind was the requirement that guilds or other business groups meet to organize standards or make plans. If transactions costs are reduced in this way, the "plans" may not be benign.

the implications of Smith's theory (Buchanan & Yoon, 2002). While the bases of trade and exchange can be differences in tastes or capacities, market institutions would develop even if such differences were negligible. The Smithian conception of the basis for trade and the rewards from developing market institutions is more general and more fundamental than simply assuming fixed, exogenous comparative advantage.

Division of labor is a hopeful doctrine. Nearly any nation, regardless of its endowment of natural resources, can prosper simply by developing a specialization. But the move to markets was no smoother, or less painful, than the move to fixed agriculture in the Neolithic. In fact, the first stages of the "industrial revolution" were very disruptive. Our modern notion of a "factory," with a production line, was startling for many.

Worse, the notion that workers must depend on other people they didn't know was unsettling. Every part of a production process must work for the resulting thing to be a "product" at all, in the sense that it can be sold. We are asking workers to trust everyone else in the whole process. And then, even if we succeed in making this enormous pile of just-one-kind – of-thing, we have to be able to sell them because we have made far more than we – or our entire city – can use ourselves.

The result was a destructive burst in productivity that quickly wiped out many artisanal trades. The expansion quickly ran up against a limiting factor: "the extent of the market." A firm specializing in making pins, or shoes, or metal items, could produce hundreds or thousands of times as much as a single artisan, so that work previously done by hundreds of skilled workers could now be done by just dozens of unskilled workers. One predictable response was industrial "sabotage," which derives from the "sabot," or wooden shoes, that hand loom workers tried to use to break the wooden gears in the "spinning jenny" or "mule" that was taking their job.[21]

---

[21] "Derives," perhaps, but the direct etymology of "sabotage" coming
from "sabot" is a bit too pat to believe. The sense of the word in French
is closer to bungling, walking noisily, or clumsily. For details, see
http://www.etymonline.com/index.php?term=sabotage.

Still, sabotage only delayed the Industrial Revolution. The increase in quality, coupled with a dramatic decline in the prices of many consumer products, ranging from small items such as brushes, knives, and flatware as well as shoes, hats, and clothing meant that traditional sources of supply were wiped out. On the other hand, by 1860 many workers were better clad and shod than members of the middle classes in 1780.[22]

[22] A famous example, early enough in Industrial Revolution to have shown a remarkable prescience, is Adam Smith's celebrated "woolen coat."

Observe the accommodation of the most common artificer or day-labourer in a civilized and thriving country, and you will perceive that the number of people of whose industry a part, though but a small part, has been employed in procuring him this accommodation, exceeds all computation. The woolen coat, for example, which covers the day-labourer, as coarse and rough as it may appear, is the produce of the joint labour of a great multitude of workmen. The shepherd, the sorter of the wool, the wool-comber or carder, the dyer, the scribbler, the spinner, the weaver, the fuller, the dresser, with many others, must all join their different arts in order to complete even this homely production. How many merchants and carriers, besides, must have been employed in transporting the materials from some of those workmen to others who often live in a very distant part of the country! how much commerce and navigation in particular, how many ship-builders, sailors, sail-makers, rope-makers, must have been employed in order to bring together the different drugs made use of by the dyer, which often come from the remotest corners of the world! What a variety of labour too is necessary in order to produce the tools of the meanest of those workmen! To say nothing of such complicated machines as the ship of the sailor, the mill of the fuller, or even the loom of the weaver, let us consider only what a variety of labour is requisite in order to form that very simple machine, the shears with which the shepherd clips the wool. The miner, the builder of the furnace for smelting the ore, the feller of the timber, the burner of the charcoal to be made use of in the smelting-house, the brick-maker, the brick-layer, the workmen who attend the furnace, the mill-wright, the forger, the smith, must all of them join their different arts in order to produce them.

(Smith, 1981, pp. 12–13)

Smith goes on to make a comparison that seems (and is) invidious, at least to modern ears. Smith compares the clothing made in mills to that worn by royalty in a society without division of labor:

[W]ithout the assistance and co-operation of many thousands, the very meanest person in a civilized country could not be provided ... what we very falsely imagine [to be] the easy and simple manner in which he is accommodated. Compared, indeed, with the more extravagant luxury of the great, his accommodation must no doubt appear extremely simple and easy; and yet it may be true, perhaps, that the accommodation of an European prince does not always so much exceed that of an industrious and frugal peasant, as the accommodation

The improvements were not immediate, however, and to many they were not obvious. Just as with the Neolithic, the Industrial Revolution had a mixed impact on the broader standard of living within the society that it had transformed.[23] Pollution and disease were appalling, as the density of population in urban areas overwhelmed the rudimentary infrastructure for managing industrial and human waste. There were enormous physical changes resulting from transportation networks (such as railroads and expanded ports) and skylines (smokestacks, enormous tenements, and extremely polluted air pouring out of the "dark Satanic mills.")[24] But these changes were not clearly benefits, at least not to everyone.

Inevitable but Not Voluntary

In this chapter, I have tried to explain why voluntary exchange and the use of markets to generate price signals are powerful forces for expanding the "cooperation horizon" for human societies. The scope

of the latter exceeds that of many an African king, the absolute master of the lives and liberties of ten thousand naked savages.

(Smith, 1981, 14)

The racism of this claim, while real, should be understood in context. Smith was arguing that the difference was based on nothing more than institutions. The English peasant was not innately superior to the "naked savages." Rather, the poor person in England had access to market institutions and a system of property rights that fostered exchange and division of labor. In principle, this success should be replicable: the institutions, not the woolen coat, would be the most important export. Any society that used markets to foster the division of labor could, in Smith's view, become "opulent" and powerful.

[23] Lucas (2002), for example, argues that the average standard of living may even have decreased slightly, though the increase in population and capacity to produce more products meant that there were far more people alive. The point is that individuals were not better off, at least not at first, particularly when accounting for the move to cities and damage to health and nutrition. City populations were much more specialized, as each person in the city was entirely dependent on someone else for food. The number of people supported by each agricultural worker in 1700 was 1.82; by 1800 it was 2.76, more than doubling in just 100 years (Harris, 2003, p. 238).

[24] The phrase is from the William Blake poem *Jerusalem*: "And did the Countenance Divine / Shine forth upon our clouded hills? / And was Jerusalem builded here / Among these dark Satanic Mills?" But it is often argued that Blake had in mind not factories but orthodox organized religion and education. In any case, the phrase is now one of the key tropes of writers describing the Industrial Revolution.

of voluntary exchange and division of labor are limited by the size of the cooperation horizon. The more people available to specialize and exchange, the greater the degree of specialization and the greater the benefits of exchange.

But the involuntary, dynamic, aggregate consequences of all these voluntary individual actions can be unexpected and harrowing. Both the Neolithic and Industrial Revolutions transformed the way that people thought of society, of goods, and of the place of people in a society that makes and uses goods. This move to towns and cities, and then to factories and large commercial enterprises, broke up cultural traditions and family connections. There was no way to go back at any stage because only a system that engaged the cooperative abilities of so many people could support so many people. Successful cooperation makes all of us dependent on each other because we come to rely on that cooperation.

What about now? How will the change in the ability to sell reductions in transaction costs and increased access to durable goods transform the cooperation horizon this time? And are the changes as inevitable, and disruptive, as those of the previous revolutions? That's the subject we turn to next.

3   The Middleman/Sharing Economy

> What is the "Sharing Economy?" ... In its simplest form, the sharing economy is composed of hundreds of online platforms that enable people to turn otherwise unproductive assets into income producing ones. These include their homes, cars, parking spots, clothes, consumer items, pets, hobbies, and many others ... Consumers are not so much interested in the sharing aspect but the cost-effectiveness."
>
> Glenn Carter, *Secrets of the Sharing Economy*

If people own stuff – clothes, tools, cars, houses – rather than rent the services that stuff provides, it means that owning secures services more reliably and at lower transaction costs than renting. But this "preference" for owning is not real. It could change quickly, if entrepreneurs could figure out a way to sell reductions in transaction costs. If I have a car, and a few minutes, and you need a ride, we can make a deal that benefits both of us. But transaction costs (the "3 TRs": triangulation, transfer, and trust) stand in the way. The value of the excess capacity in underused apartments, cars, tools, and a thousand other items is locked up. We think of it as stuff we have to pay to store, rather than stuff we could share.

It does not have to be this way. If you own something, you can extract some of this unused value by renting it out. If you own almost nothing, you can still enjoy much of the value of ownership by renting from someone else. Or you can buy something and then resell it, if the costs of reselling are low. There is a company, Poshmark.com, whose motto is "Make money from clothes that are just sitting in your closet." Poshmark does not sell clothing. It is a virtual mall, selling "space" for people to advertise clothing *they* want to sell. Poshmark sells reductions in transaction costs of access to a reliable secondary market in clothing. Buying, wearing once, and then reselling at almost the same price as the original purchase is a very useful model of "collaborative consumption." That kind of sharing is made possible by entrepreneurs selling reductions in transaction costs that would have been hard to imagine just 20 years ago.[1]

The sharing economy is

(1) entrepreneurship applied to reducing transaction costs rather than reducing production costs
(2) working through new software platforms
(3) operating on smart, portable hardware
(4) connected over a set of wifi or 2G–5G networks that are themselves interconnected (in its current form we lump all these networks of networks into "the Internet")[2]

Software programs in the sharing economy are both *system-level* (executing instructions) and *application-level* (storing, retrieving, and interpreting information entered by users). Software will play the same role in producing reductions in transaction costs that robots and automation have played in reducing production costs in the ownership economy. Software will displace human workers, reducing

---

[1] According to Felson and Spaeth (1978, p. 614), "collaborative consumption" can be described as: "those events in which one or more persons consume economic goods or services in the process of engaging in joint activities with one or more others."' For example, drinking beer with friends, eating meals with relatives, driving to visit someone, or using a washing machine for family laundry are all acts of collaborative consumption.

[2] The distinction between "wifi" (originally, in 1999, short for "wireless fidelity," though no one ever actually called it that) and NG, where the "N" is the number of the "generation" (2G is second generation; 4G is fourth generation) is likely to be blurred. But at this point the distinction still matters. 4G is slower, much more widely available, and can be expensive for large amounts of data. Wifi is very fast but restricted in availability because it is usually tied to a particular modem or antenna, e.g., in coffee shop or hotel, if you are travelling. The next – fifth – generation of cell phone internet connections should be widely available by 2020. The 5G standard requires "most" of the following (GSMA Intelligence, 2014):

- One to 10 Gbps connections to end points in the field
- One millisecond end-to-end round-trip delay
- 1000× bandwidth per unit area
- 10× to 100× number of connected devices
- (Perception of) 99.999 percent availability
- (Perception of) 100 percent coverage
- 90 percent reduction in network energy usage
- Up to ten-year battery life for low power, machine-type devices

both actual prices and implicit costs, and expanding the set of things that we think of as commodities. Software may also make a variety of new human activities, including jobs, possible for the first time. The net effect is very difficult to predict.[3]

"Analysis" means a loosening, an untying of complexity into simpler parts. To be able to analyze the likely changes resulting from the four factors listed above – reducing transactions costs using apps running on smart phones connected via the Internet – it is useful to "untie" two strands. The reason to do this is that there are two separate value propositions operating in the background, and it is easy to get confused if you do not *keep* them separate.

> Middleman Economy: Selling reductions in transaction costs to enable mutually beneficial exchange in commodities, services, and activities that may not even have been conceived as commercial until now.
>
> Sharing Economy: Making more intensive and efficient use of resources that are otherwise idle, with the consequent modification in the durable and average life of those resources as they are replaced.

The simplest way to think of how the two threads tie together was suggested by my friend Lynne Kiesling, an economics professor at Purdue University. Excess capacity means that the proportion of the time, or the capability, of the item is underused or idle, combined with the opportunity cost or foregone alternatives for which the item *could* be used during that downtime. Transaction costs are the expenses, including time, inconvenience, and actual payments required to obtain and use the item.[4]

---

[3] For example, the spread of automatic teller machines, or "ATMs," seems likely to have reduced the number of humans working for banks. Except that the number of humans working for banks, in branches and otherwise, has actually increased rather sharply (Pethokoukis, 2016). The point is that the general effects of a particular innovation are very difficult to forecast. The one thing we can forecast is that costs will continue to be driven down by competition.

[4] The movement of the relevant margin between renting and owning has been described by a number of authors. One clear presentation is that of Horton and Zeckhauser (2016), who developed a model of the ability to "share" peer to peer rather than own/rent in a hierarchy. As they note:

Table 3.1 *The Kiesling Matrix*

Level of excess capacity	Transaction Costs		
	Low	High, reducible	High, fixed
Low	Consumables and nondurables: apples		
Moderate	Already shared	Marginally profitable	Not a commodity
High	Already rented	Best value proposition	Personal (e.g., toothbrush)

The bottom right cell denotes items that are rarely used but for which transaction costs are prohibitive. Think of your toothbrush: You use it (if you are the dentist's pet) three times a day, for a total of about 4 or 5 minutes per day. For the other 23 hours and 55 minutes, it sits unused. But it is cheap, so the opportunity cost is not that high. Thus, there is no incentive to figure out ways to share toothbrushes, and no one wants to share a toothbrush the way they are now constructed. Further, the transaction cost of an arrangement where someone *could* use your toothbrush when you are not using it is pretty high. Result: Excess capacity in toothbrushes is not commodified.

The whole top row is for private goods that are consumable or nondurable. An apple, for example: I have the apple, I eat the apple, it is gone. Or a cheeseburger, or pretty much any small, discrete food item. Or a paper tissue: I use the thing to blow my

In traditional rental markets, owners hold assets to rent them out. In recent years, technology startup firms have created a new kind of rental market, in which owners sometimes use their assets for personal consumption and sometimes rent them out. Such markets are referred to as peer-to-peer or "sharing economy" markets. To be sure, some renting by consumer-owners has long existed, but it was largely confined to expensive, infrequently used goods, such as vacation homes and pleasure boats, usually with longer duration rental periods. More often, consumer-owner goods were shared among family and friends, commonly without explicit payment. In contrast, these peer-to-peer (P2P) rental markets are open markets, and the good is "shared" in exchange for payment.

(p. 1)

nose, and it is done. The transaction costs of sharing are irrelevant because the thing is so ephemeral.

Overall, things in the rightmost column are not even imagined as commodities in the first place once they are owned or used. The transaction costs of commoditizing are too high, or the rewards to changing our customs about use and sharing are too low. Of course, the only difference between the right column and the middle column is that someone has devised a way to reduce transactions costs. So things are not as static as they seem.

The bottom left cell is items with low transaction costs but with high excess capacity and opportunity cost. Very few people own cement trucks or well-drilling equipment. All sorts of construction equipment, or entertainment items like a champagne fountain for large parties and other items at "party equipment" rental shops, fit into this bottom left category.

The need to pay off a large borrowed purchase price makes the excess capacity associated with ownership risky. As Matt McLean, product manager at Volvo Construction Equipment, put it:

> Ever since the economic downturn, we've clearly seen the rental industry grow. Contractors have been hesitant to make a purchase and, quite frankly, *our culture as a whole has become more comfortable with the idea of renting versus buying – accepting a possible higher monthly payment for the gain of flexibility and risk mitigation* ... Aside from the obvious reason of financial flexibility in renting, one advantage is that *you can select the exact machine size you need for the job at hand.* With a purchase, you're looking to own a machine that will work across a variety of jobs and be a best match most of the time, with the knowledge it won't always be a perfect match for the job at hand. When renting, however, you're able to select the exact size necessary, which can then allow you to control some costs because you're not putting more power or fuel into a job that could be tackled by a smaller machine.
>
> *(ConExpoConAgg, 2017, pp. 1–2; emphasis added)*

The change does not mean that everyone will rent, but the margin where renting is an attractive alternative has shifted rapidly as transaction costs have fallen. Liam Stannard of BigRentz said,

> Ultimately it comes down to cost and convenience. If you're using a piece of gear all the time and have the resources and means to store and maintain it effectively, purchasing will probably save you money over time. On the other hand, if you're using the gear somewhat less frequently or don't want to maintain equipment storage locations and hire both service technicians and delivery drivers, then renting can be a great option.
>
> *(ConExpoConAgg, 2017, p. 1)*

The "sweet spot" for the explosion of growth in the economy of Tomorrow 3.0 is products that, and service providers who, have high excess capacity and value, but for whom current arrangements of ownership and use produce high-but-reducible transaction costs.

The reason that this is the sweet spot for new markets and new market institutions is that many of these items are not already thought of as commodities. For example, a construction firm that owns a back-hoe pays for it twice: first in the purchase price and then in the costs of storage and maintenance. But a clever app can take advantage of that latent value just sitting around. In fact, it may be "sitting around" itself that has excess capacity. This cartoon by Tony Carrillo goes further than most of us would be willing to go, but it illustrates the commodification of excess capacity pretty well. There is some price, net of transactions costs, where you would rent out a seat on your couch.

FIGURE 3.1 The Sharing Economy – A Couch Too Far?

Unsurprisingly, two of the greatest successes in the new economy are high value, underutilized durable assets: cars and housing. All you have to do is reduce the transaction costs of renting transport or shelter, and the value that was locked up until now is set free (though it's *libre*, not *gratis*). In this chapter, I will examine the nature of entrepreneurship, and then I will talk about how these two value propositions – transactions costs and excess capacity – create openings for entrepreneurs.

ENTREPRENEURSHIP

In Chapter 2 I discussed the impacts of the first two great economic revolutions, the Neolithic and the Industrial. In each case, the changes came from a new way of organizing cooperation through specialization. But the extent of the gains from specialization were limited by the horizon of cooperation. After the Neolithic Revolution, the development of cities meant that cooperation was much cheaper *within* the walls or the political boundaries of what defined the area protected (or held captive) by political power. After the Industrial Revolution, the development of the technologies of production and exchange meant that the cooperation horizon was extended well beyond the city walls, and the logic of market exchange drove the creation of institutions for reducing transaction costs for trade *between* cities, moving *across* political boundaries.

In a dynamic sense, market activity feeds back to expand the cooperation horizon. Increased division of labor pried open and integrated markets that had been segregated by distance or trade barriers. Lower production costs "want" to be global, and the result was a fundamental transformation in the way that people lived and depended on each other.[5]

---

[5] One should be careful, though. It is wrong to say that markets have nothing to do with morals. In fact, moral action is both an advantage and possibly a precondition for markets even to function. Adam Smith's argument in *Theory of Moral Sentiments* was based on conjecture, but much of the work done since (for a review, see Zak, 2011) has corroborated Smith's basic intuition.

Of course, by talking about "the logic of markets" and "division of labor" I have taken a strangely bloodless and mechanical perspective. Where is the human agency, the animating force? Perhaps the best way to illustrate the answer is an old joke:

> An entrepreneur and an economist are walking along a side street in Manhattan. The entrepreneur looks ahead, squints, and then says delightedly: "Well, I'll be darned! It's a $100 bill, right here in the street! Tell you what, I'll split it with you."
>
> The economist shakes his head and tut-tuts: "No, I'm sorry. That's impossible. In equilibrium there could never a $100 bill on the street. Someone would pick it up."
>
> The entrepreneur shrugs, and mutters, "Okay, suit yourself!" and pockets the bill.
>
> The economist looks around, and then points at the ground and yells, triumphantly: "See! SEE! I told you! There is no $100 bill."

The point is they are both right – in a sense. In equilibrium, there are no $100 bills lying around to be picked up. But that is because entrepreneurs are constantly "aware," trying to see around corners that may represent new profit opportunities. Paradoxically, then, the reason that there are no $100 bills lying around is that entrepreneurs are always looking for $100 bills lying around, and they often find them and pick them up. Economists who then say "See? SEE?" are missing the most important animating force of capitalism.

In a way, everyone is an entrepreneur, and every day each of us corrects mistakes in the environment around us. If Alice walks into a dark room and turns on the light, then the room's contents are rendered visible and so more valuable. If Alice fails to turn on the light, and trips over the trash bin, that would be a mistake.

Of course, if Alice turns on the light, she corrects a "mistake," because now resources are more usefully employed. But she creates value only for herself. In this example, the problem is reduced to decision theory: Alice has some resources – the room, the light switch – and some tasks to perform. There is no social aspect to this problem: Robinson Crusoe, alone on his island, could all by himself, discover and correct "mistakes," by moving water to irrigate crops and by using logs to build a shelter from the sun and rain. Crusoe was moving things around to create value for himself. That is an interesting problem, but it is not entrepreneurship.

Entrepreneurs must create value first for those who supply labor inputs and raw materials, paying *more* than the current owners value those inputs. Then the entrepreneur must also create value for those who buy the products or services they create, by selling for *less* than consumers value the output. If consumers willingly pay more than enough to cover all the costs of obtaining and assembling the inputs then we know that net value has been created for the society. "Profit" is the name of the reward we offer to entrepreneurs for creating value for others.[6]

The origin of the idea of entrepreneurship is contested.[7] It appears to derive from the French verb *entreprendre*, meaning "to undertake." One of the first clear statements using the modern meaning was by the economist Jean Baptiste Say:

> An entrepreneur is an economic agent who unites all means of
> production- land of one, the labour of another and the capital of
> yet another and thus produces a product. By selling the product in the
> market he pays rent of land, wages to labour, interest on capital
> and what remains is his profit. He shifts economic resources out of an
> area of lower and into an area of higher productivity and greater yield.
> *(Say, 1855, Book I, Chapter 5, p. 80).*

[6] As I discussed in Chapter 2, it is problematic simply to assume that market exchanges are voluntary, or at least that they are "truly voluntary" (Munger, 2011; Guzman and Munger, 2013). But for those who believe that all market exchange is *inherently* exploitative, the question of market entrepreneurship is not likely to be very interesting.

[7] The debate is not about when the word was first used, but rather when it was first used to mean what modern economists intend by the word. The first use was apparently in the French *Dictionnaire Universel de Commerce* by Jacques des Bruslons in 1723. But the first "correct" use may have been either Jean Baptiste Say or John Stuart Mill.

But this notion of simply buying low and selling high ignores the most important aspect of entrepreneurship: *imagining* an alternative future, creating something at the risk of destroying parts of the current reality. As Joseph Schumpeter put it: "Entrepreneurs are innovators who use a process of shattering the status quo of the existing products and services, to set up new products, new services." Schumpeter (1942, p. 83) juxtaposed two paradoxical forces to describe entrepreneurship: "creative destruction."

Israel Kirzner gives a classic description of the relation between profit, value, and entrepreneurship. You might say he explains why there are no $100 bills on the sidewalk: If prices for the same commodity differ widely, then entrepreneurs can arbitrage those differences.

> The multiplicity of prices represented opportunities for *pure entrepreneurial profit*; that such multiplicity existed, means that many market participants (those who sold at the lower prices and those who bought at the higher prices) simply overlooked these opportunities. *Since these opportunities were left unexploited, not because of unavailable needed resources, but because they were simply not noticed, we understand that, as time passes, the lure of available pure profits can be counted upon to alert at least some market participants to the existence of these opportunities.*
>
> (Kirzner, 1978; emphasis added)

Kirzner defined entrepreneurship as "awareness," the constant searching for profit opportunities. But Kirzner conceived of errors much more broadly than the above passage would suggest. Rather than simply "correcting" errors in the price system, and ensuring prices for each commodity converge to a single price, entrepreneurs imagine alternative futures, new products, and different ways of organizing production.

As we discussed earlier, this distinction is central to the working of entrepreneurship. Steve Jobs did more than arbitrage price differences; he imagined new products. As Jobs put it, "In the end, for something this complicated, it's really hard to design products by focus groups. A lot of times, people don't know what they want until you show it to them." (Reinhardt, 1998, p. 62). And Jobs was right because when he "showed them" an iPod, a solid-state device that stored digital music and could reproduce it at high quality over small ear buds, many people bought it.

Before that – the first iPod was introduced in 2001 – the Sony "Walkman" was a popular (and profitable) device that allowed people to move around or even exercise while listening to the radio or to cassette tapes. At one point, the Walkman captured more than 50 percent of the "mobile music" market. But then MP3 players were invented.[8] None of the resources needed to be invented and of the digital processes for storing the music were not especially difficult or innovative. But the package of features, the features that made up the iPod and other products like it, was something new.

The problem is that the new creation destroyed the Walkman. Sony lost billions of dollars, laid off at least 10,000 workers, and closed two large production facilities. And in a way, this harm was actually intentional because Apple had specifically *targeted* Walkman, the then-dominant product, as the consumer electronic device they wanted the iPod to displace. But that is how creative destruction works.

Until now, entrepreneurship has generally taken the form of creating products, or new productions processes, or new systems for transporting products that people want to buy. Tomorrow may be different because for the first time entrepreneurs are turning their attention entirely to a function that until now has been seen as simple, even boring. Many of the entrepreneurs of Tomorrow 3.0 will be middlemen.

---

[8] MP3 is short for MPEG 3, an abbreviation for "Motion Picture Expter Group" codings. Codings are a means of reducing the amount of information (bits of stored digital information) to encode a song without losing quality. MP3 is not the only format in which music is stored, but it has become a generic name for the subject, as soft drinks might be referred to as "coke." The first working prototype of such a player was the "IXI" created (but never produced commercially) by British scientist Kane Kramer in 1979. The first patents for MP3 encodings were issued in the US in the late 1980s and the early 1990s. The first commercially viable MP3 players went on sale in the late 1990s, and by 1999 they were relatively common in stores. The first iPods from Apple were released in January 2001; by the end of 2002, 600,000 had been sold, at prices exceeding $400 in nominal terms.

WHAT DO MIDDLEMEN SELL?

So, maybe entrepreneurs are okay. But what about *middlemen*, the folks who really do *just* take advantage of price differences? We do not like middlemen. They seem like parasites, buying products and then reselling them at a higher price, but without improving the product along the way. If they make profits, surely they do not earn them. And in fact "cut out the middleman" is a maxim of economy and prudence.

That does not make sense to me. But perhaps I'm biased because my last name, "Munger," comes from "monger," a dealer or trader, often in illicit or smuggled goods. The word derives from old Saxon, where we find it as "mancgere." Sharon Turner's three-volume *History of the Anglo-Saxons* (1836) quotes from an eleventh-century psalter:

MANCGERE: I say that I am useful to the king, and to
             ealdormen, and to the rich, and to all people.
             I ascend my ship with my merchandise, and sail
             over the sea-like places, and sell my things, and
             buy dear things which are not produced in this
             land, and I bring them to you here with great
             danger over the sea; and sometimes I suffer
             shipwreck, with the loss of all my things, scarcely
             escaping myself.

INTERLOCUTOR: What things do you bring to us?

M: Skins, silks, costly gems, and gold; various
               garments, pigment, wine, oil, ivory, and
               orichalcus,[9] copper, and tin, silver, glass,
               and suchlike.

I: Will you sell your things here as you brought
               them here?

---

[9] "Orichalcus" refers to brass.

M: I will not, because what would my labour benefit me? I will sell them dearer here than I bought them there, that I may get some profit, to feed me, my wife, and children.

(pp. 115–116; original in MS. Tib. A 3)

The mancgere cheerfully grants that he does nothing to change or improve the product. All he does is sell reductions in transaction cost, and then sells the thing at the highest price he can get. It is true that he cynically chooses to specialize in precisely those products that people will pay the most for because then the difference between the price he pays and the price at which he can sell is largest. Is not the mancgere simply preying on people's needs for goods, taking part of the surplus and providing nothing of real value himself?

Not really. Remember that from the perspective of consumers, *all costs* are "transaction costs." A transaction can only take place if the buyer will pay more than production costs plus transaction costs. The potential profit to the middleman is the offer to pay minus the offer to sell. By definition, if that potential surplus does not exceed transaction costs then the transaction is impossible. It is likely, in fact, that no one considered the possibility that there is a potential surplus from sharing in the first place. Without the middleman, there would be no "skins, silks, costly gems" or other products available. Just like Steve Jobs said, consumers do not want new stuff, until you can actually show it to them. And *then* they just have to have it.

The middleman makes possible transactions that otherwise could not take place. Transportation, information, assurance of quality through brand name, and financial clearing services are all means of making possible transactions that otherwise would be blocked by transaction costs.[10] Middlemen are crucial for making economies

---

[10] The literature on "transaction costs" is large. Key contributions include Coase (1937; 1960), Demsetz (1966; 1969), North (1981; 1990), and Williamson (1975; 1985).

work. But they are becoming even more important because selling transaction cost reduction has gotten a lot more profitable.

THE MIDDLEMAN ECONOMY

Suppose you walk through a neighborhood in New York City on a weekend in August. Or December. If you look up, you will see lots of dark windows. Apartments in very expensive neighborhoods are sometimes empty for a week or more, meaning that people are paying $600 or $1,000 per week to store dishes and furniture. But while these apartments are empty, the hotels are all full. Visitors have to stay far out of the city in New Jersey or Connecticut. If the people who want a place to stay could just find someone who has a place, or a room, a mutually beneficial exchange could be effected. But the transaction costs are prohibitive. It is hard to find a person you can trust, or to find a person who wants to pay rent for *your* apartment, or to find someone who has an apartment, or to arrange a price, or to safely and quickly arrange payment. Since the transaction costs are so high, no transactions take place.

Suppose you drive around the Financial District in Boston. If you stop at the corner of Devonshire and Milk Streets, you will notice that there are at least six enormous parking garages within two blocks. They are full, too, most days, with thousands of cars sitting there doing nothing. People pay for the car, and they pay for land to store the car. They use the car for about ninety minutes a day, and otherwise keep it in a kind of shrine, called a garage, at home or in an expensive part of downtown real estate, clogging space that could be used as a bike lane or a park or for apartments or something else.

The reason to emphasize these two types of transactions is that they are in the "sweet spot" of high excess capacity and high (but reducible) transaction costs. The reader will recognize the "sharing housing" example as the value proposition for Airbnb, and the "sharing transport" example as the value proposition for Uber or Lyft. These companies claim that they are not in (respectively) the hotel or the taxi business, but instead just operate software platforms that reduce the transaction costs of facilitating exchanges that were always possible, and always mutually beneficial, if the transaction costs problems could be solved.

The reason that Uber and Airbnb are such interesting examples is that they blur the line between owning and renting. I do not really want to own a car, I want convenient, safe, and reliable transportation services. I do not really want to own a house, I want a comfortable, anodyne, and attractive space to spend the night, or maybe a week, or five years. Renting is in many ways less expensive than owning, but people who own houses rarely rent them because of transaction costs.

To succeed, a middleman has to find a way to make money from – literally, to sell – reductions in the three key transaction costs: triangulation, transfer, and trust. To understand more concretely how these three work, let us return to the example of Uber. Uber started as a taxi company (its name, in 2009, was "UberCab"), but it is clear that Uber is actually a software company. Uber sells reductions in transaction costs.

Triangulation You can call an Uber very quickly, and both your location and your destination are handled by the software: You do not have to communicate with the driver, except through the software. Triangulation is much easier with Uber than if you have to call a taxi and get three calls from the driver who does not know the area and cannot find you.

Transfer The process of driving and paying is much easier with the Uber software. The driver does not need you to give directions because you have already provided your destination to the software, which the driver can then use to navigate while you think about something else. Of course, you may want to take a route different from that suggested by the software, but the software "sees" accidents and construction bottlenecks that you do not know about. So unless you have detailed local knowledge the transfer process is much better than the experience with a standard taxi company. Finally, after the ride is over, the driver is paid, and tipped, without you having to touch your wallet.

Trust With a standard taxi, all you can see is a small, fuzzy photo of the driver and the taxi number. You can complain about bad service, but it seems pointless. With Uber, you can take advantage of hundreds of other "pop-up" inspectors: other customers, people with accurate and up-to-date information, who leave ratings and who care about making sure other people do not have a bad experience. Further, you can see the name and license plate number of the driver, without writing it down because Uber stores it for you. You know the company has the driver's personal and financial information.[11]

The interesting thing is that there is nothing very special about using the Uber software just for transport sharing. The combination of Uber software, universal 5G wireless service, and powerful mobile smart phones can perform the same magic in a variety of other delivery and service transport arenas. Physicians can make house calls in Kansas City, bearded hipsters can make artisanal pickles for delivery in Brooklyn, and private snow plows can be coordinated by neighborhood in rural states.[12]

Of course, some of the value created by middleman-sharing platforms is the result of ducking costly regulations and avoiding

---

[11] Some people argue that Uber's (and Lyft's) safety and background checks are insufficient, and that this cheating is how they make money. But Feeney (2015) gives a detailed assessment of ridesharing safety and driver reliability. While there are some problems, he claims that they are likely to be less severe than the problems taxi drivers cause.

[12] The snow plow model is particularly interesting. It works like an "Uber Pool," which requires a group of people at some place (e.g., airport) or event (e.g., football game, concert) to cooperate and find each other. Except the software does the coordination for them. In the case of snow plows, a certain number of people must commit to paying to having the road cleared. In many cases the fact that some people "free ride" is inframarginal: If even five or six people will pay $50 to have a road cleared, it pays for the snowplow driver to provide the service. And neighborhoods can organize in advance, obtaining commitments from people they see on the street every day. Usually the problem of getting your road plowed is just transaction costs: There is plenty of demand for the service, but coordinating the bids and purchase is so difficult the service is not provided. Byrne (2016) discusses some of the incumbents in this new area, including www.plowzandmowz.com/.

taxes.[13] But that is not what is really creating value: The "middleman economy" makes its profits from selling reductions in transaction costs. Software affects the cost of services just as automation affects the cost of manufacturing. Once a platform is able to sell reductions in transaction costs, the original business model may be adapted to a variety of other activities that were unthinkable at the outset. Existing service providers may find their business models disrupted and their customers turning elsewhere, exactly like what happened to Sony and its Walkman.

AMAZON VS. UBER

There are already examples of this process, but it is easy to miss their greater significance. One obvious instance is Amazon.com. Few remember now that Amazon was originally a bookstore, the bane of brick and mortar bookstores like Barnes and Noble, or Borders, which had in their own heydays been decried as causing the death of small, inefficient "Mom-and-Pop" bookstores. Amazon provided software that allowed customers to find almost any book instantly, to pay for it using an existing account, often with "one-click" selection, and immediately send it to an address established in advance on that same account. Then the book was transported quickly and cheaply, arriving in just a few days. Later, with "Prime," it arrived in just two days, and eventually the same day.

The reason that Amazon is an important example of the Middleman/Sharing economy is not obvious until you recognize that there was *nothing special about books*; Amazon was primarily selling reductions in transaction costs. Amazon quickly expanded to a few, and then many, other products. The advantages of the reduction in transaction costs was so enormous that many sellers flocked to use Amazon's software. That software became so valuable as a means of reducing transaction costs, in fact, that Amazon began selling it directly, under the name "Amazon Web Services" (AWS).

---

[13] Koopman (2015) reviews some of the arguments for how the Middleman/Sharing economy is simply a means of avoiding taxes and regulation.

There is even a dedicated "Amazon Web Services for Dummies" book (Golden, 2013) so that Amazon can reduce the transaction cost of learning how to purchase and use their software that reduces transaction costs! AWS is a universal hosting platform that matches buyers and sellers, in a way that looks like a proprietary website for the individual seller but is in fact just a generic service robot.

That may come as a surprise to you, so let us make something clear: You think Amazon sells stuff. They do not. They license software. The way they came to this was almost accidental. In an interview with *Wired* magazine, CEO Jeff Bezos put it this way:

> Approximately nine years [in 2002] ago we were wasting a lot of time internally because, to do their jobs, our applications engineers had to have daily detailed conversations with our networking infrastructure engineers. Instead of having this fine-grained coordination about every detail, we wanted the data-center guys to give the apps guys a set of dependable tools, a reliable infrastructure that they could build products on top of.
>
> The problem was obvious. We didn't have that infrastructure. So we started building it for our own internal use. Then we realized, "Whoa, everybody who wants to build web-scale applications is going to need this." We figured with a little bit of extra work we could make it available to everybody. We're going to make it anyway – let's sell it.
>
> *(Levy, 2011)*

This is quite remarkable. It is true that Amazon originally thought of its business as selling stuff, first books and later a wide variety of other things. To be fair, Amazon is still selling a whole variety of other things, and they are building large robot-served factories to do it. But that is not where the value is. In fact, Amazon is (still) losing money as a physical seller of things.[14]

---

[14] Amazon's annual reports make it clear that the software and cloud business components of the company are where all the profits are coming from. As Richman (2016) put it:

But Amazon quickly realized that its real value was in bringing together buyers and sellers, providing a mechanism for clearing transactions reliably and safely, and providing information on sellers that outsourced trust to buyers. Amazon just needed to supply the software and the servers. People who wanted to sell, and people who wanted to buy, would self-organize into complex communities on the platform.

In fact, for many apparently proprietary web sites, it is not obvious to the users that Amazon is operating anything at all.[15] AWS is able to morph into what looks like bespoke firm web sites, reducing the transaction costs that would have prevented these companies from ever finding customers in the first place. Amazon is licensing access to AWS because software *always* has excess capacity. All you have to do is copy it and adapt it to the particular needs of a new customer.

To understand the middleman economy, one needs to recognize that the kind of disruption caused by Amazon is just the beginning. Remember, it turned out that there was nothing special about books. Likewise, there is nothing *special* about the transportation of human bodies; the Uber software is a new and extremely dangerous (to other middlemen) way to sell reduced transaction costs. Uber seems like a threat to taxi companies; it is actually a threat to Amazon. Instead of having to wait two days for your book, or your new alternator if you are working on your car, or a power drill if you are going to assemble an Ikea table, you will open Uber on your phone, and, select the

Imagine this scenario: Amazon posts a $286 million operating loss for the third quarter, its sixth losing quarter in 2.5 years. Frustrated investors call for CEO Jeff Bezos's head and punish the company's stock. Amazon defends its long-term strategy but acknowledges that it is still investing significantly to expand its business, sacrificing short-term profits. It might sound far-fetched, but that could have been the reality – if not for Amazon Web Services.

Amazon's physical sale of goods has never made a profit, and in fact is losing a ton of money every quarter. But the sale of reductions of transaction costs is doing quite nicely. Software eats the world.

[15] This is not easy to understand, and in fact many people have misunderstood, and continue to be confused. Hof (2016) gives a useful overview of the history and current dynamism of AWS. One example of this dynamism that may be familiar to fans of Major League Baseball is the participation by AWS in "StatCast," the ubiquitous analytical tool casually discussed by color commentators covering baseball games. But the reason AWS is able to provide StatCast is that they can reduce the costs of access to information to the point where it is nearly free.

product you want to rent. An Uber driver will deliver it, perhaps also taking a human passenger along the way. When you are finished you can have a different Uber driver pick up the mixer that you used to knead the bread, or the beautiful espresso machine you used after the dinner party last night. You do not have to drive, you do not have to handle money, and the rental fee is very small because the density of transactions spreads the cost of the rental item out over many renters.

Everyone has had the experience of making three trips to the hardware store to fix a faucet or a doorknob. And we all own things we would be happy to rent. The only reason we do own those things is transaction costs. New software platforms that reduce the costs of triangulation, transfer, and trust for one product or service can quickly be adapted to a variety of other products or services that none of us can foresee.[16] What is important about the middleman revolution is that the "products" are the reduction in transaction cost that will commodify activities, services, and unused resources in ways that until now have never been observed, or even imagined.

NEXT?

In this chapter, I have tried to provide an overview of the "third economic revolution," which takes the form of entrepreneurs designing software platforms that communicate over wireless connections through mobile smart phones. The "product" is the reduction in transaction costs, including triangulation, transfer, and trust. And that's good. Consumers can get what they actually want – the stream of services of durable equipment at the time and place that they want it – without having to store and maintain the durable equipment that provides that service.

The disadvantage is obvious: There will be that far fewer durable items sold because there will be relatively few cars, power drills, or sausage grinders needed at any one time, though all of them will be in use constantly. This means that the tools and products that are manufactured will be used up more quickly, of course. But that will likely lead to a focus on products that are much more durable, designed for

---

[16] Schneider (2017) provides an account of Uber as a "disruptive innovation."

the commercial rental market rather than the retail ownership market. Products will be built to better quality and durability standards because companies or individuals who will specialize in ownership will be willing to pay higher prices for products they can rent for longer periods.

Of course, the story told here misses many important elaborations or likely adaptations to reduced transaction costs. For one thing, the cheapest direction for short-term use of things may turn out not to be durables but 3-D printing, especially in remote areas. Being able to "rent" a particular form of malleable material, and then reform it into something else, would be a very different model. Even if the material itself is very expensive, I would only need to print my tool or implement, use it, and then take it back to recycle the material. But the premise is the same: I do not need to own the thing, I only need to use the thing for a little while.

Less radically, the "peer-to-peer" era of sharing I have talked about may be temporary, if transaction costs fall far enough. There is some evidence of this happening already, especially in the market for lodging. Several cities, including Reykjavik, Iceland, have found that regulations – controlling the use of apartments for AirBnb or other short-rental rental sublet facilitators – were needed to stem a drastic shrinkage in the longer-term rental market. To the "seller," the economic logic is compelling: you may only get $1,500 per month for a renter with an annual lease. But suppose you can get $150 per night for a short vacation rental, and you can average twenty nights rented per month. That is $3,000 per month. Of course, until now that second option of many, short-term rentals was blocked by transaction costs. Now, however, it is easily done.[17] There is some evidence that

---

[17] An interesting example is described by Kristen Brown (2016):

One Airbnb host in Reykjavik told me that converting a rental unit he owned had provided him and his wife with income to save for retirement – something he could never afford to do renting the property out annually.

"We make maybe two to four times the money depending on the time of the year," said Heimer Fridriksdottir, who owns one Airbnb unit and is a janitor. "If it's our apartment, it should be up to us who we rent it to. The city should just build more apartments."

people are buying up entire buildings, giving the current tenants non-renewal notices at the end of their leases, and then converting all those units (in effect) to hotels, with Airbnb operating the front desk and reservations line.[18]

Regardless, whether the sharing is peer-to-peer or a hierarchical and specialized ownership-rental arrangement, what all that means is that far fewer people will be employed in manufacturing these items, and jobs will be lost. It seems likely that this bug is actually a feature, of course. Or better, an example of Bastiat's "broken window" fallacy.[19] The "lost" jobs are in fact just expenses not incurred, as it becomes possible to acquire the services of items over time and then return them so that someone else can use them. It is clearly true that the transformation will be disruptive, as each of the previous great revolutions disrupted patterns of exchange and civic organization. Like those other revolutions, the result may be an initial decline in quality of life as the costs of transition are paid. But the real bottom line is that, like it or not, the change is coming. The logic of markets selling reduced transaction costs to commodify excess capacity is irresistible.

[18] For recent models of the peer-to-peer market and some regulatory dimensions, see Akbara and Tracognab (2018), Einav et al. (2015) and Horton and Zeckhauser (2016).
[19] The "broken window" fallacy derives from Bastiat's (1848) observation that making things cheaper appears to cost jobs, while destruction (such as a broken window) creates jobs. but the problem is the difference between the "seen" (the glazier making and installing the window) and the "unseen" (the other uses that would have been made of the resources). Having much cheaper products and less storage needs will have real benefits, though the specifics are often unseen.

4 The Answer Is "Transaction Costs" – Uber Sells Triangulation, Transfer, and Trust

"Disruption" describes a process whereby a smaller company with fewer resources is able to successfully challenge established incumbent businesses. Specifically, as incumbents focus on improving their products and services for their most demanding (and usually most profitable) customers, they exceed the needs of some segments and ignore the needs of others. Entrants that prove disruptive begin by successfully targeting those overlooked segments, gaining a foothold by delivering more-suitable functionality – frequently at a lower price. Incumbents, chasing higher profitability in more-demanding segments, tend not to respond vigorously. Entrants then move upmarket, delivering the performance that incumbents' mainstream customers require, while preserving the advantages that drove their early success. When mainstream customers start adopting the entrants' offerings in volume, disruption has occurred.

Christensen et al., "What Is Disruptive Innovation?"

Until now, throughout the Neolithic and Industrial Revolutions, disruption has taken the form of making new stuff, better stuff, or being able to deliver stuff to new places. And transaction cost has played an important but subsidiary role in this process. Several Nobel Prize winners in economics, including Ronald Coase and Douglass North, worked on understanding transaction costs. It happens that Doug North was one of my dissertation advisers in grad school. At my thesis defense, Doug asked a question. It seemed complicated, and I'm an economist, so I went to the board and wrote some equations to stall. Finally, (mercifully) Doug interrupted. Waving his hand slowly, as if to a not-very-bright child, he said, "Michael, the answer is ... transaction costs!"

It took me several years to realize, and more than a decade fully to understand, that for Doug North it did not really matter what the question was. The answer always starts with "transaction costs." The reason it took me so long to fully understand this perspective is that – unexpectedly, if your focus is on traditional economics – Doug was right.

STUFF IS IN THE WRONG PLACE: RONALD COASE AND EXCHANGE

All over the world, "stuff" is in the wrong place. That's why people exchange: I want something you have more than you want it, and you want something I have more than I want it. If we exchange, we'll both be better off, even though there is no more stuff than before. Why is stuff in the wrong place? The answer is "transaction costs."

I rent a large (10' × 20') storage unit, and I pay nearly $200 per month rental. In that storage unit, there is – among many other things – an almost-new outboard motor. No boat; just a motor. That motor is worth $1,000, which is quite a bit of money. But I spend $1,200 every year just to *store* it. Why?

By now you know the answer: transaction costs. Or, to put it another way, organizing exchange is expensive. The father of "transaction costs economics," Ronald Coase, began his life as an economist because he was puzzled. The question that puzzled him seems obvious, but once you start to think about it the way Coase thought, it changes everything. In an interview, Coase put it this way:

> We were discussing the way that businesses were controlled, and their plans were made, and all that sort of thing. On the other hand, [professors] told us all about the "invisible hand," and how the pricing system worked itself, and you didn't need any plans and so forth. It seems quite natural to me now, though it doesn't seem to have bothered many other people: [H]ere you had these two systems operating simultaneously. One, within the firm, a little planned society, and on the other hand relations between firms conducted

through the market. And yet, according to the way people looked
at it, the whole thing could have been done through the market.

(Coase, 2002)

Economists always go on and on about the price system and its magic.
But it markets and prices are so great, why are there firms? But then, if
firms are so great, why is there not just one big firm?

Coase's answer is now standard in economics: Firms will expand
or shrink until the cost of "making" equals the cost of "buying." Of
course, this is not true on every margin: Very few company cafeterias
grow their own wheat, but the Carnegie Corporation purchased mines
to ensure that it had reliable access to the iron and coal it needed to
make steel. Interestingly, Krause (1992, p. 173) describes a situation
where Andrew Carnegie misjudged the correct "make-or-buy" margin,
purchasing some ovens near Larimer in east Pittsburgh to guarantee
access to coke for the steel: "By the 1880s, it was costing Carnegie more
to operate [the coke ovens] than to buy all his coke from an independent source. It was an unacceptable situation." So Carnegie sold off the
ovens and bought his coke on the open market. The firm shrank
because of a change in transactions costs as production became more
standardized and reliable. Changes in transaction costs will often affect
the boundary between make or buy, and the size of firms will change –
perhaps quickly – as innovations in transaction costs management
become available.

Interestingly, the Coasian analysis applies equally well to what
seems like a very different question: Why do we own things, rather
than rent? As you know well by know, I am claiming that the answer
is transaction costs. But the ways that transaction costs – triangulation, transfer, and trust – are costly tells us a lot about the problem. It
involves time.

TRANSACTION COSTS – AND TIME

In Chapter 3, I mentioned the fact that many people own power
drills, but rarely use them. Why would this be true? The answer is

"transaction costs": It is cheaper, even with the costs of having money tied up in the drill, and having to store the drill, to own rather than to rent. Because renting is extremely inconvenient.

What this illustrates is that the notion of "transaction costs" cannot be defined precisely because costs depend on the particular circumstances of time and place for that commodity and that transaction. It is tempting to define transaction costs as all the costs of completing a transaction *other than* the costs of producing the good or service being sold, but even that would be a mistake. The notion of separating the good itself from the way that it is produced or sold requires ownership, but all most people want is the service the durable good can provide.[1] Again, from the perspective of the buyer, *all costs are transaction costs*. I do not care whether the reason the product is "expensive" is that it is expensive to produce or that I have to stand in line a long time to arrange to use it. Those are both costs that the consumer figures into his or her decision.

Some observers (see, for example, Cairncross, 1999) have focused on the importance of improved communications technologies and network economies in communications devices. But computers and smart phones are just the platforms on which the actual cost reductions, and the rapid expansion of transaction density, depend. Being able to consummate complex transactions without fear of fraud or robbery is more than a change in "communications"; it is a reduction in the cost and risk of renting or sharing services in ways that have never before been possible.

---

[1] A much deeper version of this discussion is given in O'Driscoll and Rizzo (1996). One of their significant contributions is to point out that the constant adjustments of entrepreneurs who hold durable commodities as a store of value will depend on the "cost" of such inventories, but these costs themselves are constantly in flux based on expectations of the ability to have alternative uses for the commodities. The ability to rent a durable when it is not actually being used dramatically reduces the costs of ownership. Who will own what, and how much? There is no way to know. As O'Driscoll and Rizzo put it, "This indeterminism is typical of evolutionary processes." (p. 193).

Likewise with the crowdsourcing of trust: It is not just *information* that is now being more cheaply transmitted. The software platforms of the future generate new information, specific trust-enforcing mechanisms in the form of reviews or surveys, where before there was no reliable metric other than word-of-mouth reputation. Crediting communications technology with embodying everything important about the transaction cost revolution is as misleading as crediting electricity for innovations in personal computing. The communication technology is necessary – but not sufficient – without entrepreneurs who could realize the potential of that technology.

MIDDLEMEN AS BROKERS AND SELLERS OF CONNECTIONS

The middleman sells reductions in transactions costs, at a price much less than the transactions costs being replaced. This in turn makes possible transactions that otherwise would never happen. Transportation, information, assurance of quality through brand name, financial clearing services – all of these are means of making possible transactions that otherwise would be blocked by transaction costs. Companies that specialize in renting complicated commodities, such as cars, have figured out ways to reduce the transaction costs dramatically, both those faced by consumers and those faced by the company.

It happens that the author is a "member" of a particular auto rental software platform; it does not matter which, so let's call it "Entavertz."[2] This means that when I exit an airplane my phone buzzes immediately. Software has sent me a text, with the exact location (say, "Slot C18") of "my" rental car. Of course, it is not really mine, because I am renting it. But that's the point: It's the car that I want, or rather the car I would want if I had to think about it. My preferences for auto type, identification, insurance, gas option, return date, and payment are all already known by the software. All I have to

---

[2] "Entavertz" is a portmanteau of "Enterprise, Avis, Hertz." It's not a real company.

do is walk directly to the car I want to rent, which has my name on the electronic screen above it and the keys waiting inside. The only actual person I see is the guard who checks IDs at the exit gate. All of the other aspects of the transaction are handled behind the scenes, and (from my perspective) instantaneously, by software.

All this discussion of renting cars harkens back to the earlier point: Why do we rent some things (cars) but buy others (power drills)? I do not really want to own a car; I want convenient, safe, and reliable transportation services. I do not really want a drill; I want a hole in this wall, now, right here. The difference is that someone has figured out a profitable way to sell reductions in transaction costs for renting cars but not power drills (yet).

To succeed in the new economy, entrepreneurs must find ways to sell reductions in transaction costs, somehow licensing or otherwise capturing part of the value of all those newly enabled transactions. When I give versions of my academic lectures on the Middleman/Sharing economy, I always start with my argument that the answer to every question is "transaction costs," just like Douglass North said. But then I continue the lecture, and after a few minutes I ask if anyone hitchhiked today to get to the lecture. People look at me as if I'm crazy; "*nobody* hitchhikes nowadays," their faces seem to be saying.

So, I'll call on someone. I always call on a young lady, someone sitting near the front of the lecture hall. The reaction is always the same: "No! No, I didn't hitchhike."

I ask, "Why not? Why don't you hitchhike?"

How quickly they forget. The answer is usually something like, "It's creepy!" or "It's too dangerous." But the answer to this question, like almost every other important question in explaining economic decisions, is "transaction costs."

Of course, this little routine only works if I try it in the United States. In Europe, or Asia, or Africa, or Australia, nearly half of the young people in the lecture hall would raise their hands when I asked if any of them hitchhike. Because they all know about BlaBlaCar.

RIDE-SHARING

There is no better way to tell the story of the origins of "ride-sharing" than to quote from the BlaBlaCar "Home" webpage:

> BlaBlaCar was born one Christmas, when founder Frédéric
> Mazzella, a student at Stanford, wanted to get home to his family
> in the French countryside. He had no car. The trains were full.
> The roads, too, were full of people driving home, alone in their car.
> It occurred to him that he should try and find one of the drivers
> going his way and offer to share petrol costs in exchange for use of
> an empty seat. He thought he could do it online, but no such site
> existed ... The adventure had begun!
>
> Fred had imagined a new transport network built on people, that
> could bring efficiency to road transport, solve congestion problems,
> make travel affordable and social. With a background in scientific
> research (he studied physics and later worked at NASA) he saw the
> full potential of a peer-to-peer transport network, and the huge
> environmental and economic benefits of enabling a more efficient
> use of existing resources.
>
> *(www.blablacar.co.uk/about-us/the-blablacar-story)*

Unlike many of the other forms of software platforms, BlaBlaCar is *pure* sharing. The software provides information about the location of someone who wants a ride and the destination of someone who has an extra seat in their car or truck. Even after the BlaBlaCar company takes its payment, the driver spends less on a trip he was taking anyway, and the passenger spends less than the cost of a train or driving or any other means of transport available. The result is a pure efficiency gain, with close to zero marginal cost to the system, but benefits to all three participants.

Charmingly, the name of the software platform comes from a parameter that is matched for customers – "Chattiness." If you prefer a quiet ride, and drive, then "bla" riders can be matched with "bla" drivers. But if you cannot keep quiet, and love to talk the whole trip, you can select "bla-bla-bla" (or "Won't shut up!") and both passenger and driver can chatter the whole way. The name of the company selects the middle setting, "bla-bla" (which the British version characterizes as "Enjoys a natter") as the way to represent the service overall.

The success of BlaBlaCar shows the truth of Steve Jobs' claim (from Chapter 3) that "A lot of times, people don't know what they want until you show it to them." But that's exactly what BlaBlaCar has proved. As McGauley and Cole (2016) noted:

> At first, the prospect of an app that basically makes it easier to hitchhike seems absurd. This is something no one is asking for, right? But here's the rub: the app is already a huge hit. . . in Europe. It's called BlaBlaCar, and it matches up passengers who need long-distance rides with drivers who are already headed that way.
>
> *(p. 1)*

As of this writing, BlaBlaCar has well over 25 million "members," in twenty-two countries. At least 10 million trips are arranged per quarter, and of course each "trip" requires at least two members, driver and passenger. In fact, the average car occupancy is 2.8 in a BlaBlaCar ride, compared to 1.6 to 1.8 (depending on the country) for car trips in general. BlaBlaCar estimates a reduction of CO_2 emissions on the order of more than 1 million tons per year, but of course that assumes that all riders would have taken their own trip solo, rather than take a train or simply not travel, if the service were not available.

Lots of people wonder why BlaBlaCar has not entered the US market. It appears that the answer is the lack of mass transit in US cities makes pure city-to-city travel less valuable, because the rider has to take a taxi or Uber at the other end anyway. There are some small scale but similar apps, such as Zimride, WeFlok, Rdvouz, or Poparide, but BlaBlaCar itself has not yet tackled the potentially enormous US market.

Notice the recurrent theme here: BlaBlaCar does not sell rides, or transportation, or anything remotely like a physical service. What BlaBlaCar sells is a reduction in transaction cost. When Frédéric Mazzella needed a ride, and noticed that there were hundreds of cars and trucks on the highway with empty seats, he had a transaction cost problem, or rather three problems.

Triangulation The passenger and the driver needed to find each other. They needed information about where the passenger was located, where the passenger wanted to go, and where the driver was headed. They needed to arrange a time and location for the pick-up, and that time and location had to be convenient for both (not far from the passenger, and on the route the driver was going to be traveling anyway).

Transfer The software must organize the transaction in a way that is nearly costless. Having both the passenger and the driver use smartphones means that there are three aspects of transfer that are much cheaper than with having to deal with a physical transaction. First, the phones have GPS, so they "know" where they are and where the other phone is. Second, if there is a mix-up, or a problem with location, they can call or text each other. Finally, the payment can be negotiated by the software (based on a standard formula), and then actually transferred from one account to another wirelessly, without having to handle cash, make change, or haggle.

Trust Trust, or the "creepiness" factor, is the primary reason why hitchhiking is so rare in the United States. Traditionally, the triangulation problem was solved by standing by the road with a thumb up, announcing the desire for a ride. And transfer was solved by having the rider stand on an entry ramp or by the side of the road in the direction of the desired destination. Those are not great solutions, but they worked well enough that hitchhiking was once fairly common, reasonably efficient, and very cheap as a way of traveling.

As Steve Levitt put it, on the *Freakanomics* radio show:

> Hitchhiking is a classic example of what an economist would call a matching market where there's a person who wants a ride, and there's a person who's willing to give a ride, and there's actually usually typically no money changes hands, so somehow there are people getting benefit on both sides of the transaction. The fifties, the sixties, maybe even the seventies, there was some sort of

equilibrium in which there was a set of people who wanted to hitchhike, and there was a set of people who were willing to pick them up. And somehow that equilibrium got destroyed. So the question is what happened to the equilibrium?

(http://freakonomics.com/2011/10/10/
where-have-all-the-hitchhikers-gone-full-transcript/)

The answer is actually not clear. There was the "bad hitchhiker" in fiction, as in the movie Texas Chainsaw Massacre. There was the "rapist driver" in reality, as in the bizarre case of Colleen Stan, imprisoned and tortured from 1977 to 1984. But in terms of actual probabilities, there is little evidence that hitchhiking became much more dangerous.

But "trust," or the lack of it, clearly increased the perceived transaction costs of hitchhiking, which became much less frequent. Instead of trying to hitchhike, travelers used other systems. And instead of picking up hitchhikers, drivers rode alone.

Software can "crowdsource" trust. The software itself does not provide the information; what happens is that many people independently record their experiences and perceptions, and what emerges is a powerful – and valuable – signal about reliability. Older people seem to want regulation, or some tangible source of trust, but younger people are used to relying on crowdsourcing. If you are in a strange city and you are looking for a restaurant, you do not ask the hotel concierge (who is likely to recommend a restaurant that bribed him), and you do not look at the local Health Department ratings. Young people use Yelp, or some similar software program that sells reductions in transaction costs. Negative reviews are quite damaging but informative.

The system is not perfect, but it is quite good. The key point is that BlaBlaCar, and other systems such as Uber and Airbnb, depend on their ability to crowdsource trust. The stakes are much higher than choosing a restaurant, of course, but the system still works. Remember: the software records the identity and financial information of all parties, and it provides a time-stamped record of all their interactions leading up to the actual transaction. It is certainly possible to fabricate an identity, but then it is possible to fake an employment record and work for a taxi company or a hotel. Customers, whether driver or passenger, know much more about their counterparts using BlaBlaCar than in the analogous situation of a shuttle or taxi driver.

Mazzella, founder of BlaBlaCar, recently created a whimsical character called "Trustman" (www.betrustman.com/). More formally, the crowdsourced trust solution is based on the D.R.E.A.M.S framework: "Declared, Rated, Engaged, Activity-Based, Moderated, Social, networks for trust." Mazzella calls it "collaborative consumption," and that's really a key insight. According to the Trustman web site:

> Today, we read and write reviews and ratings about just about everything: holiday destinations, restaurants, consumer goods, even people. And we trust these peer reviews: [R]ecent studies show that 75 percent of people trust them, against only 45 percent who trust advertising. These online ratings record trust and make it publicly available to everybody across the globe, at any and all times. The result is that the radius of trust has been radically enlarged to include everyone online. It's what is enabling fast-growing sharing economy (a.k.a collaborative consumption) businesses like Airbnb and BlaBlaCar. Thanks to online profiles, we are now free to share or rent essential resources like cars or accommodation, to swap items, houses and skills, to crowdfund and crowdsource, to massively collaborate . . . all of which not only saves us money and time but actually makes all our lives richer.

Now that we have considered a variety of examples superficially, it is useful to consider one example in depth. One of the best examples, partly because it is so controversial, is the ride-sharing service Uber.

UBER: HERO, VILLAIN, AVATAR

One of the clearest, and most vilified, examples of the middleman economy is Uber. We talked about Uber earlier: If I have a car, and a few minutes, and you need a ride, we should be able to make a deal that benefits both of us. But we cannot, because transaction costs are too high. For a very long time, the solution has been a specialized service provider, the hackney carriage, jitney, or taxi. The problem of needing a ride is generic, and ancient. But taxis are expensive, sometimes difficult to find or contract with, may be dirty, and may have drivers who are abusive, and drive aggressively. The costs to the consumer are the sum of the costs of waiting, the inconvenience of having to give directions, of having to pay, and the terror of being driven in a hurtling missile whose operator is hanging out the window screaming at other operators doing the same thing. So when someone says "Taxis cost too much," they may not mean just monetary costs.

To be fair, it is no picnic *driving* a taxi, either. The work involves long hours, often spent waiting or driving around without a fare, and passengers are often abusive. Worse, some "passengers" turn out to be robbers or thugs; drivers are exposed because they sit in the front with the customer behind them, mostly out of sight. In 2000, the federal Occupational Safety and Health Administration (OSHA 2000) issued a report that cataloged the many dangers of driving a cab, ranging from exposure to assault to physical problems. As driver advocate James Szekely put it:

> I ask people if they would spend a day picking up total strangers and taking them wherever they wanted to go. They tell me, "No, that's dangerous, that's insane, you'd have to be on drugs!" But somebody got to do it – we can't all be doctors or lawyers. We're called service workers, and we deserve protection.
>
> (Quoted in Kloberdanz, 2014)

Almost everyone has a story. Here's mine: My older son lives on New York's Lower East Side. When we visited, we always took a yellow taxi from La Guardia airport. One visit, a few years ago, we told our taxi driver the address, and he nodded. Off we went ... heading north, to the Kennedy bridge. That's a very long way to go. The driver pretended not to speak English and managed to do a loop up around Columbia University, far off the best route. I protested, but the driver just shouted at me and my wife in a language I did not recognize.

When we finally got to our son's apartment, after ninety minutes of aggressive driving and being rocked around, I asked if I could pay with a credit card. The driver immediately learned some English, and said, "Of course, I help!" He hopped in the back seat, took my card, ran it through the slot and then quickly gave himself a 50 percent tip. I objected, but he said, "Look, I wait long at airport, okay? Have nice day." He got back in his seat, and popped the trunk lid, waiting for us to get our own luggage out of the trunk.

I could not give the driver a bad review (just as drivers cannot give obnoxious passengers bad reviews). And even putting aside problems with obnoxious or unscrupulous drivers, it can be very difficult to find a taxi, in cities such as New York, San Francisco, or Paris. Once, after waiting at a taxi stand for forty minutes in Paris, we decided just to take the Metro, even though it meant walking half a mile in the rain at both ends of the trip. That beats having to wait an indeterminate time in the rain.[3]

That's really the story of Uber. Taxis cost too much. For both passengers and drivers.

Uber: The Creation Story

Like most creation stories, the tale of Uber has an air of myth. But the central fact is that restrictions on availability, and the cost of employing drivers full time, made taxis in the San Francisco and Silicon Valley area both expensive and ridiculously inconvenient.

---

[3] If you have ever wondered why you cannot find a taxi when it is raining in New York City, here is one explanation: on rainy days and nights, drivers get more fares much more quickly. That means that they make their "income target" early, and they just go home. If the price could adjust upward, they would have some incentive to stay out. But without a price increase to offset the increased scarcity, you are not going to get a taxi. (Jaffe, 2014).

It reminds me of the old line about restaurants, adapted to cabs: "The price is way too high, but at least you can never find one!"[4]

One version of Uber's creation myth is given by Travis Kalanick (2010). Kalanick claims that he and Garrett Camp, while attending a "LeWeb" conference in snowy Paris in 2008, stayed up most of the night (as they often did, having fairly recently sold their own web start-ups, StumpleUpon for Camp and Red Swoosh for Kalanick) "jamming" on ideas for a new venture. They kept coming back to how terrible taxis were as a way of getting around, particularly in San Francisco. As Kalanick (2010) put it, "getting stranded on the streets of San Francisco is familiar territory" for those who live there.

The original idea –remember, these guys were really rich, and busy– was a kind of limo timeshare, selling the use of a few hours of a driver, a $140,000 Mercedes S-class, and a parking spot in a nearby garage. They laughed at the idea that they could write an iPhone app that would sell pieces of this service on demand whenever the driver was on duty.

Of course, they quickly figured out that the way to create value was not in buying the car/driver/garage combination and selling pieces of it. The big innovation was the software platform that would allow people to "sell," and others to "buy," pieces of cars that were owned by regular folks. Still, they expected that the business would be "low-tech, mostly operational." They began a "test run" in New York City in January 2010 around SOHO/Union Square, and worked on making the system efficient and less buggy. They had to make up almost everything from scratch, since the model they were trying to replace – subvert, actually – used fixed pricing, physical maps, line-of-sight hailing, company-owned cars, and analog phones. To switch to a software-operated, GPS-based, automatic charge processing, and dynamic pricing system with "volunteer" drivers supplying their own cars was a massive conceptual reinventing.

---

[4] The Groucho Marx version (which is likely apocryphal, but is mentioned in *Annie Hall*, is: "The food is terrible here. And such small portions!" (1977).

The team (with Camp taking a smaller role but new recruit Ryan Graves stepping in) scheduled a limited launch in San Francisco for May 31, 2010, with a full live launch in July. By the end of 2010, just seven months later, hundreds of drivers had signed up and thousands of passengers had paid for rides. In 2011 Uber expanded to many US cities, and in 2012 it began a limited extension to other countries, beginning with France and the UK.

In 2013 Uber launched in South Africa and India; in 2014 international expansion began in earnest, with more cities and new service in China, Nigeria, and other countries. By January 2018 Uber was operating in nearly 1,000 cities in more than 80 countries worldwide, with more than 1.50 million rides each day. The total number of drivers is hard to specify, since the very nature of Uber is part time and voluntary for many drivers, rather than full time and compulsory for people with jobs. But it is safe to say that there are 500,000 Uber drivers in the United States and well over two million worldwide.

Uber Is Not a Taxi Company

The Uber software reduces the transaction costs of triangulation, transfer, and trust in local transportation, but there is no reason to expect that "taxi" function to be primary for long. There are many other kinds of goods and services for which the particular combination of location, connection, payment, and reputation that Uber provides will prove valuable.

In fact, that's already happening. Here are some of the activities into which Uber has expanded:

- UberHop: Something like a bus service. People going in a direction can catch a ride, but can get on and then get off as part of the ride. In Seattle, for example, a driver can move along one of 14 fixed routes in a van, picking up passengers and letting them.
- UberCommute: Something like organized hitchhiking. If someone is driving on a route anyway, traveling to work, that driver can pick up and drop off other travelers or commuters who are going the same way at the same time, for a fee.

- UberRush: In effect, this works exactly like regular Uber, but what is being delivered is products instead of human travelers. It is much faster than other delivery services, and the software makes the door-to-door delivery much easier on both ends.
- UberBoat: Water taxis. Lots of people have boats, and regular water taxis are very expensive in places such as Venice or Istanbul. But with Uber . . .
- UberFresh/UberEats: Food delivery, either from grocery stores or from restaurants. Delivery is a losing proposition for most groceries and restaurants because they do not do enough volume. But with the Uber software to handle the connection and payment, lots of people are happy to pay for convenient delivery, allows groceries and restaurants to focus on their own core businesses.
- Washio: Dry-cleaning and laundry. Again, the advantage is partly in the ability to call a driver, but it is also convenient to have the payment handled seamlessly.

So let's summarize: Uber is a software platform. Uber the company sells reductions in transaction costs, making possible a wide variety of transactions that otherwise would not take place. We have never noticed the transactions that do not take place because it is hard to imagine a world where people can make money by selling reductions in transaction costs.

But that is precisely the world of Tomorrow 3.0: Things that until now have been liabilities can become assets. If you have a bike, but you are leaving college for the summer, you'll need to pay to have it stored. Unless . . . you can find someone who wants to rent it. Instead of you paying someone to keep the bike, denying its use to the world, you share the bike and make money instead of paying money. That's "SpinLister."

Or, suppose you have to be out of town for three days, and you are thinking of putting your dog in a kennel, something that costs you money and your dog hates. What if someone wanted to have a dog for just a few days? That's "BarkNBorrow" There are plenty of people who would like to have a dog to play with for a weekend, and your dog gets nice walks instead of being locked in a cage.

PROBLEMS WITH DISRUPTIVE TECHNOLOGY

There are two problems with Uber, or anything "Uber-like." One is fairness, and other is economic disruption. It is easy to conflate them because people usually try to use justice to defend their self-interest. But let's keep them separate. I'll take up the fairness argument later in the chapter; for now, let's focus on disruption.

There is some debate over whether Uber is a "disruptive technology," in the sense intended by Christensen et al. (2015). If all it does is take over the taxi industry with a slightly better business model, then the nay-sayers are right and it is not truly "disruptive," at least in the terms described in the quotation at the beginning of this chapter. Existing forms of economic organization resist disruption, sometimes fiercely, and—at least by their own narrow, possibly anti-social object-ives– quite rationally.[5] What economists call "disruption," after all, is

---

[5] This distinction between general purposes, installed in rules, and narrow objectives, installed as corporate or organizational strategies, is not always appreciated. As Adam Smith (1981, p. 250) argued:

> The interest of the dealers... in any particular branch of trade or manufactures, is always in some respects different from, and even opposite to, that of the public. To widen the market and to narrow the competition, is always the interest of the dealers. To widen the market may frequently be agreeable enough to the interest of the public; but to narrow the competition must always be against it, and can serve only to enable the dealers, by raising their profits above what they naturally would be, to levy, for their own benefit, an absurd tax upon the rest of their fellow-citizens.
>
> The proposal of any new law or regulation of commerce which comes from this order ought always to be listened to with great precaution, and ought never to be adopted till after having been long and carefully examined, not only with the most scrupulous, but with the most suspicious attention. It comes from an order of men whose interest is never exactly the same with that of the public, who have generally an interest to deceive and even to oppress the public, and who accordingly have, upon many occasions, both deceived and oppressed it.

Douglass North argues that:

> A crucial distinction in this study is made between institutions and organizations. Like institutions, organizations provide a structure to human interaction ...
> Conceptually, what must be clearly differentiated are the rules from the players. The purpose of the rules is to define the way the game is played. But the objective of the team within that set of rules is to win the game ... Modeling the strategies and skills of the team as it develops is a separate process from modeling the creation, evolution, and consequences of the rules."
>
> *(North, 1990, pp. 4–5)*

hundreds of people losing their jobs forever because the jobs no longer exist in anything like the same form.

When cars were being introduced, the people who made buggies and took care of horses reacted by trying to pass regulations that made cars impossible, or at a minimum so inconvenient that the cars would be blocked, and their use would be curtailed and restricted. A famous example is this regulation from 1896, passed (unanimously!) by the Pennsylvania General Assembly. The regulation is an example of a "red flag" law; the name comes from the requirement, found in many cities in the United States and England, that any self-propelled vehicle be proceeded by a man on foot (on foot, mind you!) walking 50 to 100 feet in advance, waving a red flag in warning.[6] Here is a summary of the Pennsylvania bill, which was passed by the legislature but vetoed by Governor Daniel Hastings: Any car

> upon chance encounters with cattle or livestock to (1) immediately stop the vehicle, (2) immediately and as rapidly as possible disassemble the automobile, and (3) conceal the various components out of sight behind nearby bushes until equestrian or livestock is sufficiently pacified.
>
> *(Karelovitz, 1968, p. 122)*

Why would such a silly law be passed? It's certainly possible that legislators were reacting to legitimate concerns about safety, since the new technology seemed dangerous. But much of the problem with the new technology was that it was just new. In 1915 there were nearly 27 million horses and mules in the United States (and only 100 million people). By 1970 there were fewer than 5 million horses and mules in the United States, though the number has rebounded a little since then.

---

[6] Originally, the laws were used to restrict and inhibit locomotives, on tracks, but later were used to obstruct progress in transportation in general. Typically, any self-propelled (as opposed to horse, ox, or mule-drawn) vehicle was required to arrange for a person on foot, walking along waving a red flag. Sometimes, a noise maker – a whistle, or drum – was also required, though presumably the sound of a steam or internal combustion engine was, in those primitive levels of development, quite enough warning on its own.

The skills and resources required to train, feed, house, ride, and otherwise make use of horses at the turn of the twentieth century were very valuable. In fact, there is a cliché that has become a part of the language on economic disruption: the "buggy whip maker." Buggy whip makers are, in the argot of scorned business failures, manufacturers or service providers who fail to recognize that times are changing, or who find that their once-valuable skills are now obsolete.[7]

Overall, the replacement of expensive skilled labor with more productive machines or software is valuable. Economic competition implies the replacement of inferior systems of production and distribution by more efficient mechanisms. Better ideas work through killing off the old ways, the old firms, and the old jobs. But this "replacement" is brutal for those being replaced. Instead of "survival" in a biological sense, the competition is over providing goods and services at higher quality and lower cost. Consumers win, in this system, but it is tough on workers. At least 5 million people – saddle and tack makers, trainers, stable owners, manufacturers of buggies and coaches, and so on – lost their jobs when horses were largely replaced by cars, trucks, trains, and ships. (Greene, 2008, p. 175). Estimates range from 5 million to 10 million jobs lost in the next decade as a result of the new disruption from the sharing economy. (Shavel et al., 2017, p. 4).

Why so much destruction? It is tempting to blame management because "buggy whip makers" – and their modern heirs – fail to foresee the changes in their industry. That would have required quite a bit of foresight, of course. In fact, Henry Ford is said to have pointed out that consumers themselves cannot foresee fundamental changes, even though consumers drive the changes: "If I had asked consumers what they wanted, they would have said 'Faster horses!'" If

---

[7] Interestingly, there is some question whether the buggy whip simile is even remotely historically accurate. See Strossjan (2010) for background.

consumers cannot foresee change, how can the businesses that serve consumers forecast change?

The (apparent) origin of the "buggy whip" simile/metonymy is Theodore Levitt, in a famous (though controversial) essay in the *Harvard Business Review* in 1960.[8]

> Every major industry was once a growth industry. But some that are now riding a wave of growth enthusiasm are very much in the shadow of decline. Others that are thought of as seasoned growth industries have actually stopped growing. In every case, the reason growth is threatened, slowed, or stopped is not because the market is saturated. It is because there has been a failure of management.
>
>   The railroads did not stop growing because the need for passenger and freight transportation declined. That grew. The railroads are in trouble today not because the need was filled by others (cars, trucks, airplanes, even telephones), but because it was not filled by the railroads themselves. They let others take customers away from them because they assumed themselves to be in the railroad business rather than in the transportation business.
>
> *(Levitt, 1960, p. 45)*

> ... [T]here is no guarantee against product obsolescence. If a company's own research does not make it obsolete, another's will. Unless an industry is especially lucky, as oil has been until now, it can easily go down in a sea of red figures – just as the railroads have, as the buggy whip manufacturers have, ... and indeed as many other industries have.
>
> *(Levitt, 1960, p. 50)*

Levitt's claim is probably simplistic, but the "what business are we in?" question is at the heart of the world of Tomorrow 3.0.

And that's really the punch line of this chapter: The reason that Clayton Christensen's claim at the start of this chapter is wrong – and it

---

[8] It is a metonymy because the buggy whip manufacturers stand in for the whole – the many industries disrupted by the replacement of horses with other kinds of power and transport.

is quite wrong – is that Uber understands that it is not in the transportation business. It is in the business of selling reductions in transaction costs, using a software platform connected over the Internet and accessed through smart phones. But the folks who currently think they are in the transportation business are going to try to keep Uber out.

BUGGY WHIP MAKERS OF THE WORLD UNITE: THE UMPIRE STRIKES BACK

When it comes to a battle among technologies and products for the affection of consumers, we tend to think of the state as a judge, a kind of umpire. But sometimes the umpire plays favorites. The California Labor Commission, an administrative law body, issued a ruling on June 16, 2015, which reclassified Uber drivers from contractors to employees (Munger, 2015a). This had several effects, but the short version is that the costs of having employees rather than acting as a seller of information will effectively prevent Uber from expanding, and may even cause it to pull out of California altogether.

The point is that taxi and livery drivers just don't understand what business they are in. They think they sell transportation, but in fact they sell reductions in transaction costs in finding and paying for transportation services.

And they do an increasingly bad job of that, compared to the new competition. That is why Uber has been so successful. Uber itself is not a transportation company; it is just a platform for connecting a willing buyer and a competent, nearby seller who has some extra time. If you think that Uber is a transport company, you are one of Levitt's "buggy whip makers," someone who does not understand what the real value proposition is.

In any kind of fair contest between Uber and traditional taxi companies, software eats the old way of doing things. But the umpire struck back, first in California and then in Texas. The "workers" who drive Uber often do it precisely because they can set their own hours and they have the freedom to decide whether to offer rides on any particular day or route.

The California "court" (which is not a court at all but the Labor Commission) said this, in response to the suit by disgruntled driver Barbara Berwick):

> Defendants hold themselves out as nothing more than a neutral technological platform, designed simply to enable drivers and passengers to transact the business of transportation. The reality, however, is that Defendants are involved in every aspect of the operation.
>
> (California Superior Court, 2015)

Wow. That's like saying that Rotten Tomatoes makes movies. What Rotten Tomatoes (www.rottentomatoes.com/) does is to provide information about a transaction (buy a movie ticket to movie X, to movie Y, or stay home) that will take place only if the consumer decides they want to see that movie, or not. Yes, Rotten Tomatoes is "involved" in the movie watching business, pretty deeply. But what they are selling is information.

Of course, it really is true that with Uber (unlike with Rotten Tomatoes) you pay the company, and they pay the driver. But the rates are fixed and known in advance (yes, even during a "surge"). Uber just acts to clear the transaction conveniently and quickly, so you do not have to carry cash and neither does the driver. It is just not true that Uber is paying the driver. The passenger is paying the driver in a way that is more convenient for everyone. Uber just handles the transaction.

The problem is that "the rules" do not allow for adaptation to changing circumstances. Professor Levitt blamed management for being unable to understand "what is your real business?," but regulators make the problem even worse. By definition, it is hard to make profits or provide services in an industry that does not exist. And if political decisions are based on votes, it will always be true that there are more existing jobs depending on obsolete technology than there are votes from workers whose jobs have yet to be created.

The reason that traditional employee-driven (pardon the pun) transport services are disappearing is that software is cheaper, faster, and better than "employees," from the perspective of consumers. Taken as a whole, the costs to traditional taxi consumers of paying more, ranging from monetary costs to transaction costs of various kinds, is far higher than the benefit to employees of keeping their jobs. But the costs to consumers of preserving the "buggy whip" version of transport is widely dispersed. In fact, it may be invisible because much of the cost takes the form of transactions that do not take place.

The real solution is for the umpire – in this case, the state – to quit playing the game and to go back to a neutral role. Sure, it is tough to see one side get crushed, especially when those workers are willing to contribute almost any amount of money and time to the cause politically. The losing side loses completely. Their jobs are gone, and they will not come back. It takes a very strong-willed politician to pass up the short-term benefits of protecting dying industries, when those industries will pay anything you ask.

What makes Uber, and other such technologies, invincible in the long run is the underlying *economic* logic. The political benefits to protection reflect the short-term bias of politics, where no one can see past the next election. Still, the economic benefits to technological disruption will always win in the long run.

FIGURE 4.1 The Inevitability of Sharing

A Different Example: "Uber but for Planes"

If I'm a pilot, and have my own plane, and I'm planning to fly from San Francisco to Portland, Oregon, it would be easy for me to carry an extra passenger and a normal amount of luggage along with me. The fixed costs (the airplane, maintenance, insurance, my license and experience as a pilot, and landing fees) are already paid. The additional cost would be the small amount of additional fuel because of the extra weight.

But, of course, it is hard for me to find someone who wants to go from the same place, to the same place, at the same time. It is hard for us to get together, and to arrange the payment. And I am not sure I want to fly with someone I do not know because they might rob me or just be crazy and creepy. My problem is transaction costs.

What we need is (this will sound familiar) a software platform that does those three things, and does it very fast and without effort by either the pilot or the potential passengers. The developers of a web site called "Flytenow" realized that it could make money by selling reductions in transaction costs in a kind of "Uber, But For Planes" arrangement. In a way, this is more like our earlier discussion of "Blah-Blah-Car" in central Europe because this is a trip that the driver/pilot was going to take anyway. So if the price is equal to the marginal cost, plus just a little, both passenger and pilot are better off.

But, the umpire strikes back. The US Federal Aviation Administration imposed new regulations in early 2016, ignoring the fact that "flight sharing" is already widely used, and quite safe, in Europe.[9] According to one analysis (Meyer, 2016), the existing regulations allow flight sharing, as long as it is not solely for profit and "the pilot and the passenger share a common purpose." It certainly sounds like "I want to go to Portland, and so do you" is a "shared purpose."

---

[9] In January 2017, the US Supreme Court formally declined to review the lower court rulings that upheld the FAA's interpretation of the statute. And in fairness, the Court is likely correct: the law really does require the FAA to act this way. For more, see Coyle (2017), and Koopmans and Dourado (2017).

Furthermore, if I am charging only the marginal cost I'm losing money on the trip, unless I wanted to go there, anyway.

Perhaps the most interesting thing about the new regulations is that the restrictions apply only to "meeting" over the Internet, using a web site or social media such as Facebook. Flight sharing via physical bulletin boards, or making an announcement at a luncheon with 600 guests is fine; you just cannot use the Internet! Reminds one of Frederic Bastiat's (1996) "Negative Railroad,"[10] where the point of regulations is to raise costs to benefit existing producers.

That's the point of sharing: We make more efficient use of existing resources, and trips that are already being paid for, while making services available to people who might not otherwise be able to afford them. As one of the founders of Flytenow, Alan Guichard, put it:

> [S]pecial interests are at the heart of it. The FAA is being pressured by lobbyists in the private charter and airline arena to ban flight sharing. Why? Because flight sharing gives people options – sharing a flight from Boston to Martha's Vineyard costs less than $70, whereas a charter would cost at least $1,000. These established business models see flight sharing as a threat.

[10] Bastiat's "Negative Railroad" example goes like this:

> M. Simiot raises the following question: Should there be a break in the tracks at Bordeaux on the railroad from Paris to Spain? He answers the question in the affirmative and offers a number of reasons, of which I propose to examine only this:
> There should be a break in the railroad from Paris to Bayonne at Bordeaux; for, if goods and passengers are forced to stop at that city, this will be profitable for boatmen, porters, owners of hotels, etc.
> Here again we see clearly how the interests of those who perform services are given priority over the interests of the consumers.
> But if Bordeaux has a right to profit from a break in the tracks, and if this profit is consistent with the public interest, theAngoulême, Poitiers, Tours, Orléans, and, in fact, all the intermediate points, including Ruffec, Châtellerault, etc., etc., ought also to demand breaks in the tracks, on the ground of the general interest – in the interest, that is, of domestic industry – for the more there are of these breaks in the line, the greater will be the amount paid for storage, porters, and cartage at every point along the way. By this means, we shall end by having a railroad composed of a whole series of breaks in the tracks, i.e., a negative railroad.
> *(Bastiat, 1996, pp. 94–95)*

... According to the FAA, it is perfectly okay for *strangers* who meet over a physical bulletin to share a flight, but if those same people meet online, where flight-sharing services such as Flytenow offer *verified identities*, then the flight magically transforms into an illegal commercial operation.

(Quoted in Meyer, 2016)

This is pretty remarkable. It is precisely *because* the Uber-style software platform allows people to find each other, to make payments, and to trust each other – i.e., reduces transaction costs – that it is prohibited. Less efficient, less effective ways of matching passengers and pilots pass the gimlet eye of the regulator; the problem is precisely that software works better.

Resistance Is Futile, and Yet ...

At the time of this writing, there have been riots, protests, and legal controversies in several major cities in the United States, including Austin, TX, Eugene, OR, and Las Vegas, NV. And there are even bigger problems and protests in Paris, France; Fukuoka, Japan; Bogota, Colombia; London, England; and even normally free-market oriented Santiago, Chile. A recent AP story about events in Santiago sums up the two sides pretty well:[11]

Thousands of Chilean taxi drivers protested against Uber's application [to do business in Santiago]. They accuse Uber of taking nearly half of their customers, and causing traffic chaos in the main streets and parking areas of Santiago and other cities ...

Despite opposition to [Uber], more and more riders who have switched said Uber has newer vehicles, called conveniently and quickly by a software app, that the fare is known in advance, and that the identity and photograph of Uber drivers are known. Further, Uber is much cheaper than traditional taxis; in some

[11] See the original AP story, in Spanish, which I edited slightly in translating at http://hosted.ap.org/dynamic/stories/A/AMS_GEN_CHILE_UBER_SPUS-?SITE=AP&SECTION=HOME&TEMPLATE=DEFAULT&CTIME=2016-05-12-12-27-09.

cases the difference is around 50%. Also, it is not necessary to
pay with cash, because the software records your credit card when
you enroll.

... By contrast, some taxi drivers tamper with their meters,
resulting in illegally high charges; keep their vehicles in dirty or
dangerous condition; and are sometimes verbally abusive
to customers.

The author of that news story seems sympathetic to Uber, and
the customers who are choosing Uber must prefer its service. How
could anyone protest? Are not the taxi drivers just being selfish?

In political economy, you should probably never think of someone as "just" being selfish. The reasons why people do things are
complicated. It is true enough that taxi drivers are being harmed,
but let's look at it from their perspective: the taxi drivers saw a set
of rules, and played by them. Now, a new company is coming in, and
claiming the rules (registration, licensing, use of meters) does not
apply to them. At a minimum it seems like a problem of "equal
protection under the law," does it not?

Let's consider an example, one where the notion of property rights
is clearer. It happens that I own about 35 acres of forest land, a "tree
farm" with around 20,000 loblolly pines. Imagine that one day I go down
to my property, and as I walk around I hear chain saws and trucks. They
sound pretty close, so I walk into the property to investigate.

About two hundred yards back in the woods I come across a
group of men, cutting down trees and using loaders to put the trees on
trucks. I demand to know what they are doing. The men smile and
say, "Oh, you must be the owner. We understand that you are angry.
But our concern is for consumers. If we can avoid having to pay all
those taxes, and buy the land and pay for upkeep and fertilizer, we can
sell this wood for a much lower price than you could ever afford to sell
it. You just don't understand economics! It's all about the consumer!"

Well, they are right. I am angry. And I may not understand
economics, but I understand cell phones. So I make a phone call.
And quite quickly several heavily armed men show up, and confront

the loggers, pulling out their guns if the loggers do not immediately stop their operations.

Friends of mine? Vigilantes? Absolutely not. These armed men also have badges, badges that say "Deputy Sheriff, Alamance County." The reason is that I am a landowner, and taxpayer, in Alamance County. Specifically, I have a piece of paper that gives me "property" in this piece of forest. That paper is a title, and it is careful to specify the exact boundaries of the property. As with any property, this paper gives me two rights: The first is the right of use, meaning those are my trees. The second is the right to exclude, meaning those are not your trees, or anybody else's trees, because they are my trees.

The loggers are rounded up and hauled away, their equipment is confiscated, and they are forced to pay me in civil court for the trees they cut. They also are charged with *criminal* trespass and theft, a charge brought not by me but by that county because theft is a crime against the entire society. They may not go to jail, but they are in pretty serious trouble because I had a promise from the government to protect my exclusive rights to use those trees.

What about their argument that consumers would be better off? It is probably true, is it not? After all, the price at which the illegal loggers could sell lumber would be far lower if they do not have to obey property rights, pay taxes, or observe regulations. But that's the point: the reason the trees are there, and in general the reason why people invest in taking care of property and factories is that "property" gives them the right, and the power of the police gives them the ability, to guarantee that they can profit from those investments.

Are taxis really any different? Consider the situation in New York City, on Manhattan Island. According to the ordinances of the city, a taxi driver, or "hack," must obtain access to a "medallion," a metal tag physically riveted to the hood of the car, with a corresponding piece of paper (a "title," in effect).[12] The taxi industry in the city was regulated, but not limited, until 1937. Over time, about 11,800

---

[12] See Meyer (2016) for a short history of the medallion system in Manhattan.

medallions were sold at auction. If someone wanted to get out of the taxi business, he could sell the medallion. The prices of medallions, both in auctions and in secondary markets, rose to at least $300,000 each, and spiked as high as $1 million dollars at times in the 1990s.

The idea of using medallions to raise money, and to restrict the number of taxis in Manhattan, may or may not have been good. The rationale for imposing the medallions as a restraint on entry is complex, but it has three parts in general. The first is to prevent over-crowding (Manhattan is a small, and crowded space); the second was to raise revenue for licensing and enforcement by selling the medallions; the third was to ensure high quality and good service by restricting low cost or "fly by night" gypsy cabs.

But regardless of whether the government *should* have created and promised to defend a semi-exclusive right – only people who have medallions can drive taxis – the government *did* make that promise. And taxi owners ponied up, in good faith. Since then, the market price of the medallions has reflected the value of that promise. Other people purchased them on the secondary market, again in good faith. If you have a medallion, you can operate a taxi (use right), and if you do not you cannot operate a taxi (exclusion right for owners of medallions).

Why is the title to my forest land entirely different from the medallion? In both cases, the buyers paid for a bundle of rights, and one part of that bundle was the promise of the government to protect those rights. After all, the philosopher John Locke was surely right when he said,

> For a man's property is not at all secure, though there be good and equitable laws to set the bounds of it, between him and his fellow subjects, if he who commands those subjects, have power to take from any private man, what part he pleases of his property, and use and dispose of it as he thinks good.
>
> *(Locke,* Second Treatise, *chapter 11)*

You might argue that my right to my forest land is a property in tangible things, and the state is simply securing that right. The difference would then be that the medallion was an artificial, and in fact made-up, right that had no basis in physical property. But that would be true of many financial, or "intangible," assets. More importantly, it seems odd for ardent defenders of property to blithely assert that the government should decline to enforce rights, paid for in good faith, if those rights happen not to please a temporary majority. In fact, that protection of rights against confiscation by majorities is exactly the function of the "takings" clause of the Fifth Amendment to the US Constitution.[13]

Whatever else Uber is doing, it is providing private transport services in Manhattan. It is plausible to think that this reduces the value of the medallions that were sold based on a promise that no one could provide private transport services in Manhattan without a medallion. And, in fact, the decline in price is clear, with sales of medallions recently at $200,000 or less, down by 80 percent or more from their peak. Do we owe taxi drivers compensation for the loss of value of the medallions?

The answer might come down to the difference between a full "taking" and a "regulatory taking," under the Fifth Amendment. "Takings" are the full transfer of a property right to the state, for public use. But "regulatory takings" are the reduction in value from the loss of some rights to property. The Endangered Species Act, for example, leaves the owner with his or her property rights intact, except that no use can made of the land if it disturbs the species being protected.[14]

The point for present purposes is that regulatory takings are not compensated, under the interpretation of the Fifth Amendment adopted by the judicial system. Taxi medallions are "regulatory givings," a valuable rent that involves protection from competition. The value of the "giving" was always variable, and the buyers should have expected

---

[13] "No person shall … be deprived of life, liberty, or property, without due process of law; nor shall private property be taken for public use, without just compensation."

[14] In the Supreme Court case *Palazzolo v. Rhode Island*, 533 U.S. 606 (2001), it was held that a buyer of land can challenge regulations that reduce the value of the land. But in this particular case it was also held that there was no actual "taking" because the regulation had been capitalized in the value of the land when it was paid for.

that a politically created rather than physical right was of less perman-
ence, and of more risk, than other assets.[15] So taxi medallions are
different from physical property.

Just as no guarantee is made to Sony to protect the Walkman
from MP3 players, no guarantee is made to medallion owners that
new forms of competition will be foreclosed. But there may be nonetheless a political impulse to offer some compensation, in effect
buying out the medallion owners, to make the transition to the better
solution (something like Uber) smoother and faster.

Surge Pricing

There is another objection many people have made to Uber and other
middleman economy software companies based on their pricing prac-
tices. Several incidents have enraged voters and attracted the attention of regulators. Perhaps the most famous was the aftermath of a
terrorist attack in Sydney, Australia's Central Business District (CBD)
in December 2014.

Uber's fares are generated by an algorithm that takes into account
location, the number of riders hailing cars, and the number of cars in
the area (though not the distance between the car and the potential
passenger). The algorithm serves at least two important functions: First,
it "rations" access to rides: if there are more riders than rides, some
system is necessary for deciding who gets picked up. Second, the algorithm raises fares received by drivers in a way that attracts more drivers.

---

[15] And in fact, as Van Doren (2014) shows, the price of medallions appears to have had
a risk discount for exactly this possibility. Vany (1975) famously analyzed the
technical economic conditions of a taxi system with medallions as an entry
restriction, and they showed that the regulated meter price would have to be set
very high (inefficiently high, in terms of marginal cost of providing the service) to
induce sufficient levels of service. Then, since entry is restricted because of the
medallion system, the cost of medallions is artificially inflated to obtain access to
the right to charge these grossly inflated prices. The point is that the regulated
meter price under a medallion system can be adjusted to obtain efficient
levels of service. The problem is that the deadweight costs of artificially high meter
rates – excessive wait times and taxi rides not taken – are very substantial.

These counterbalance, at least in part, the rationing problem by making more rides available at times of peak demand.

Note the elegance and simplicity of the price signal: drivers do not need to know *why* there is a shortage of cars in an area. All they need to know is that if they drive to that location and pick up passengers they will be paid a premium.

Which brings us back to Sydney. A terrorist had taken thirteen people as hostages, and thousands of people in the CBD were desperate to get away. There were not nearly enough taxis and buses for everyone to leave at once; the bridges leading out of the CBD were clogged.

Many people were stranded. The only cars and vans entering the CBD, crossing the bridges toward the danger were Uber drivers. Hearing that there was a higher price than usual, Uber drivers left their apartments, got in their cars, and drove to where people needed rides.

Let's stop for a moment and consider two people: Willy and Zach. Willy is an Uber driver who hears of the higher price, and drives into possible danger in the CBD to provide a ride to a desperate person who wants to get out. Zach is Willy's next-door neighbor, watching the hostage crisis unfold on Australian Broadcasting Corporations Channel 2. Zach feels great sympathy for the people in the CBD, and he stays glued to the television all afternoon. Willy drives into the CBD and provides transport to passengers. Who is more morally admirable?

Strangely – and this is very strange, when you think about it – most people think Zach, who does nothing but has feelings of honest sympathy is more moral than Willy, who actually gets in his car and drives into danger to provide a service people actually need. Uber was castigated furiously for using price as a means of getting help to people who needed it. One user, Matthew Leung, said "I have never, ever seen it at four-times [the normal rate] and I'm a 1 percent top Uber user ... I understand the way the business works – higher the demand, higher the charge – but four-times at $100 minimum is ridiculous. Almost price gouging at its worst."

The accusation sounds pretty bad: Greedy Uber took advantage of the desperate need of people to escape, and raised prices to make more money. But in fact, that's not what happened. The only people who knew about the terrorist/hostage event were people like Zach, watching TV. All Uber's algorithm knew is that suddenly, in the middle of an afternoon, thousands of people all tried to take Uber rides at once. The algorithm tried to match passengers with rides. The only way to do that was to raise price, to attract more drivers.

The frustrating thing is that the algorithm worked the way it was supposed to. There were enough rides that people actually got into cars. Of course, they noticed that the surge meant the price was high. But the alternative was not to have a ride at the usual low price, but to have no ride at all, at any price. The desperate riders would still have had to pay, but they would have paid in the form of higher transaction costs: longer wait times and much more trouble finding a ride. Surge pricing is always with us; it is unavoidable. The only question is whether to make it a money cost or a queuing and inconvenience cost.

TRANSACTION COSTS: A DIFFERENT WAY OF THINKING OF "SURGE PRICING"

One of the key elements in making a decision to buy a good or service is the transaction costs involved in actually making the purchase. A useful way of defining transaction costs is this:

Transaction costs = Final price – Production costs

One could quibble that some of the costs paid by the producer are also transaction costs. But the advantage of this simple definition is that it makes clear that transaction costs drive a wedge between the amount received by producers ("production costs") and that paid by consumers ("final price").

From the perspective of the producer (in this case, a taxi driver), the costs include the rental of the car, the "rental" of the medallion, the value of the time spent in the taxi, and the costs of insurance and so on.

From the perspective of the consumer (the potential rider), the costs include all of the producer costs (because the driver will only be there if they are making a profit). But the final "price" also includes:

- Triangulation: You have to find a cab, or call a dispatcher and wait for the cab. When it is raining, or if the dispatcher or driver misunderstand your location, this can take a very long time.
- Transfer: You have to endure the conditions of the trip and find a way to pay for the trip.
- Trust: You have to believe that you will not be robbed or subjected to verbal abuse or threats as well as accept the risk of aggressive or dangerous driving.

The most obvious problem is waiting time. If you have trouble finding a taxi, the dispatcher or driver have trouble finding you, or you have to wait (as is common) forty-five minutes or more for a ride, which is a real cost. The cost to the passenger is the sum of the fare, the wait time, the risks of the ride, and the inconvenience of having to negotiate and pay the fare.

That all means that the medallion/meter system – by restricting entry and price adjustments – imposes surge pricing every bit as uncompromising as Uber's algorithm:

Consumer price = meter price + wait time + search/payment costs

In times of high demand, the "rider" has to wait longer, to make repeated phone calls to the dispatcher, or stand in the rain waving at already-full taxis. Is it not better to have the price rise than to have the transactions costs rise? The interesting thing is that the *total* price (paid by consumers) is the same either way because price always – *always* – rises to clear the market. The difference is that rationing by wait time and inconvenience is inefficient and wasteful. Consumers "pay" waiting costs, but producers do not receive the value of the wasted time.

Most people have never thought this through, but it is just basic economics. *Consumers "pay" the same amount, regardless of whether surge pricing is allowed.* The only question is whether the "surge" takes the form of higher money prices or higher transactions costs in the form of longer waits and greater inconvenience. We have surge pricing now, and we have always had surge pricing. Just ask someone who has tried to get a taxi in Manhattan or Paris or London at 7:30 p.m. on a rainy Saturday night: You can pay with money, or you can pay with time; either way, surge pricing just happens.[16]

So, there's the real answer to the question I posed earlier. Uber exists because the founders of the software platform figured out a way to sell reductions in transaction costs. And the "surge pricing" problem is just as bad with the medallion/meter system. The only question is whether it is better to pay "surge" prices by waiting and searching for a ride by standing in the rain on a busy street and waving your arms like an idiot. Those are costs, too, and in a time of shortage those costs increase to match the number of passengers and the number of available taxis.

Maybe you think that's okay. But surge pricing based on money does something else, something crucial: it actually increases the supply of the service at just the time when people need it. The problem with "surge pricing" based on varying transaction costs is that it provides no incentive to offer more of the service.

Uber is not a taxi company. It is a software platform that sells reductions in transaction costs. Surge pricing is essential to that function. Most importantly, there is no reason that it needs to deliver humans to locations. More and more, Uber and other things that are "Uber, but for _____" will be delivering things to humans.

---

[16] In 2012 my son Kevin Munger was living in Santiago in Chile. I visited, and we went to have dinner in the lovely Bellas Artes neighborhood. After dinner (which in Santiago means 11 p.m.) it started to rain. It was about a kilometer to the Metro stop, and it was raining fairly hard. We approached a taxi, and the driver quoted a price that was at least triple the meter rate. We were outraged and decided to walk instead. We noticed that the couple behind us got in the cab, which then sped past us. Did the driver behave badly? He certainly broke the law, but consider: he was sitting there precisely because he knew that there was no nearby Metro stop. And the couple behind us valued the ride more than we did, so the fact that we said "no" meant that the ride was available for the higher value users. If the driver had stuck to the regular meter fare, we would have taken it, which would have been inefficient since we valued the ride less than the people behind us. But if the driver were scrupulous and stuck to the meter fare, he likely would already have been at home, since the meter fare is not enough to provide the service of sitting in some neighborhood at 11 p.m. Surge pricing is great, even when it's illegal.

5 Jobs, Work, and Adaptation

> We are suffering just now from a bad attack of economic pessimism.
> It is common to hear people say that the epoch of enormous economic
> progress which characterised the [previous] century is over ... that a
> decline in prosperity is more likely than an improvement in the decade
> which lies ahead of us.
>   I believe that this is a wildly mistaken interpretation of what is
> happening to us. We are suffering, not from the rheumatics of old age,
> but from the growing-pains of over-rapid changes ... The increase of
> technical efficiency has been taking place faster than we can deal
> with the problem of labour absorption.

J. M. Keynes (1930, p. 194)

The passage above was written on the eve of the greatest worldwide economic *collapse* in modern history. If "we" were suffering from pessimism, we had reason to be.

Nonetheless, history has vindicated Keynes's optimism. And Keynes's description of the *causes* of pessimism – we have already grown all we can, standards of living will stagnate, our children will be worse off than we are, and so on – sound so familiar. He identified a problem he called *technological unemployment*.

> We are being afflicted with a new disease of which some readers
> may not yet have heard the name, but of which they will hear a
> great deal in the years to come – namely, technological
> unemployment. This means unemployment due to our discovery of
> means of economising the use of labour outrunning the pace at
> which we can find new uses for labour. But this is only a temporary
> phase of maladjustment. All this means in the long run that
> mankind is solving its economic problem ... Thus for the first time
> since his creation man will be faced with his real, his permanent
> problem-how to use his freedom from pressing economic cares, how
> to occupy the leisure, which science and compound interest will
> have won for him, to live wisely and agreeably and well ...

Yet ... we have been trained too long to strive and not to enjoy. It is a fearful problem for the ordinary person, with no special talents, to occupy himself, especially if he no longer has roots in the soil or in custom or in the beloved conventions of a traditional society ... Three-hour shifts or a fifteen-hour week may put off the problem for a great while. For three hours a day is quite enough to satisfy the old Adam in most of us!

... There are changes in other spheres too which we must expect to come. When the accumulation of wealth is no longer of high social importance, there will be great changes in the code of morals. We shall be able to rid ourselves of many of the pseudo-moral principles [such as a focus on wealth and possessions to confer status] ... by which we have exalted some of the most distasteful of human qualities into the position of the highest virtues ... I look forward, therefore, in days not so very remote, to the greatest change which has ever occurred in the material environment of life for human beings in the aggregate.

(Keynes, 1930, pp. 358–359)

Keynes's prediction that people might work less, and perhaps much less, as a result of increased productivity has not yet been proven correct. There is little evidence that people in wealthy countries work less, or that wealthy individuals in most countries work less (in fact, they work *more*).[1] If this continues, the biggest differences in income and living standards will not be between the wealthiest and poorest nations, but between wealthy people almost everywhere and poor people almost everywhere. As the transaction costs barriers of distance and physical proximity are stripped away, there will be is nothing left to protect the least able, and the least educated, in very wealthy nations.

---

[1] Kuhn and Lozano (2008) show that average workweeks go up with increasing wealth of a nation, and that within a nation higher-paid workers, even if they are salaried, work longer hours. Cowen (2013) and Murray (2012) claim that there may be some movement in the direction that Keynes envisioned, but that the disparity in the magnitude of the change is causing problems.

Consequently, in the world of Tomorrow 3.0 we should expect profound disruption. One kind of disruption, called *saltation*, is mostly – though not entirely – good, because it means that the institutional and legal preconditions for development in poor nations will no longer be necessary. Software will allow even a nation with a corrupt government and police force, rudimentary banks and broken capital markets to leapfrog the usual drawn-out development process and to produce useful services.[2] The other kind of disruption, which we might call *separation*, is mostly – though not entirely – bad, because it means that many people will be left behind, in most cases through no particular fault of their own, and will be relegated to second-class status in wealthy nations.

I will consider each of these two types of disruption and their likely effects. But before we do that, we need to step back and think a little bit about the history of work.

DISRUPTION: ECONOMIC REVOLUTION

The two great economic revolutions of the past, the Neolithic and the Industrial, smashed the cultural traditions and identities that people had used for centuries to organize their social lives. The Neolithic Revolution replaced hunter-gatherer identities with specific, often hereditary occupations The family of the metal-worker was named "Smith," the merchants were "Mongers," the barrel-makers were "Coopers," the candlemakers were "Chandlers," and so on.

The 1840s were a time of great disruption and upheaval, and the commodification of products that had once been produced by artisans or in the home meant that now money was required to acquire the basic necessities of life. The initial stages of the Industrial Revolution

---

[2] Leeson and Boettke (2009) note that entrepreneurship can take place also at the level of institutions. The interesting thing about technologies such as Bitcoin is the ability to facilitate such innovations and avoid obstructions, intentional or otherwise, from local authorities or the lack of state capacity. See also Boettke, Coyne, and Leeson (2008).

destroyed many of the traditional systems for distributing goods and services, and they were not smoothly replaced. This was the period in which the notion that workers had "jobs," as opposed to identities, first became possible. As labor was "commodified," the idea of labor itself was separated from the laborer. Karl Marx was pessimistic about this separation arguing that it is more like what we would now call "human trafficking."

> [T]he fact that labor is external to the worker [means that] it does not belong to his intrinsic nature ... He feels at home when he is not working, and when he is working he does not feel at home. His labor is therefore not voluntary, but coerced; it is forced labor. It is therefore not the satisfaction of a need; it is merely a means to satisfy needs external to it. Its alien character emerges clearly in the fact that as soon as no physical or other compulsion exists, labor is shunned like the plague. External labor, labor in which man alienates himself, is a labor of self-sacrifice, of mortification ...
>
> As a result, therefore, man (the worker) only feels himself freely active in his animal functions – eating, drinking, procreating, or at most in his dwelling and in dressing-up, etc.; and in his human functions he no longer feels himself to be anything but an animal.
>
> *(Marx, 1844, p. 30)*

Marx had a key insight: In an industrial system focused on production, the position of the citizen is first and foremost a provider of labor.[3] One might lament, or celebrate, this commodification of work hours, but it is an input to the machine of industrial capitalism, as well as being caused by commodification, a system where most products and services can only be obtained through the price mechanism.

Marx's focus on labor as the only source of value is rather misleading, even apart from being bad economics. The real problem

---

[3] Marx's discussion of the pressure to reduce costs through automation – which now means software – as a driving force of the form of production in vol. III, chapter 5 of *Capital* (Marx, 1992) certainly appears prescient.

of economics is recognizing that the only thing that drives economic evolution is the consumer. Market systems are mechanisms for facilitating cooperation, cooperation among people who own things, people who make things, and people who want things. And the commander of the system is the consumer. As Ludwig von Mises put it:

> The real bosses, in the capitalist system of market economy, are the consumers. They, by their buying and by their abstention from buying, decide who should own the capital and run the plants. They determine what should be produced and in what quantity and quality. Their attitudes result either in profit or in loss for the enterpriser. They make poor men rich and rich men poor. They are no easy bosses. They are full of whims and fancies, changeable and unpredictable. They do not care a whit for past merit. As soon as something is offered to them that they like better or that is cheaper, they desert their old purveyors. With them nothing counts more than their own satisfaction. They bother neither about the vested interests of capitalists nor about the fate of the workers who lose their jobs if as consumers they no longer buy what they used to buy.
>
> (Mises, 1944, Book I, chapter 1)

The clearest exposition of this concept, and the most useful for our purposes, is that of W. H. Hutt (1940). Hutt points out that there are two different loci of direction and control: The *choice of ends* rests with consumers; the *choice of means* rests with producers (and to a lesser extent, workers). More simply, consumers decide what gets made; business and labor decide how it gets made, subject to the constraints imposed by competition. One of the central themes of this book echoes Mises above: Consumers have no deep commitment to any particular thing, or way of delivering value. They will choose based on their whims and (importantly) the transaction costs of using the thing to obtain the value consumers seek.

Consequently, if business can find a way to deliver *products* (until now, purchased and owned by the consumer) in the form of a *service* (a rental delivered and picked up at low cost, or operated by someone else), that form of delivery may replace all the other systems for delivering that product. The system is not designed to create jobs, it is actually focused on destroying them, if that's what consumers want. And that, was essentially Marx's ethical criticism of capitalism. Marx failed to understand the wealth of new ways that new jobs would be created, but he was quite right that competition almost always leads to job destruction.

The question is whether the what has worked in the past – leave things alone and new jobs and entire new industries will be invented – will still work in the new system. Until now, to consume, you had to work. The value of the things you could buy in the market were limited by the value of the labor you had to sell. But if consumers can rent or share rather than own and store, it may soon be possible to consume while working much less. Keynes foresaw the reasons: enormous changes in productivity, driving down prices. The fundamental human economic problem, scarcity, will be solved, for many kinds of goods. But Keynes was not a Marxist; he did not think that "late capitalism" would immiserate labor. To the contrary, Keynes thought the effects were mostly *positive* because the costs of things would fall by even more than nominal income.

Consider two online social media platforms, Facebook and Twitter. Both of these offer free access to "customers," or people who sign up to use the platform. How much value do Facebook and Twitter produce? The usual way of thinking about it, in the era of the manufacturing economy, is to use the notion of GDP, or Gross Domestic Product. The value is the new thing that is produced, and sold for a price. In this case, that would be the *revenue* social media companies take in from advertising. GDP is the total money value of all transactions taking place in the economy. It is (ignoring international trade):

$$GDP = \sum_i^n p_i x_i$$

where p_i is the price, and x_i is the quantity, of the "i"th good. Obviously, if $p_i = 0$ it counts nothing toward GDP, regardless of how much consumers subjectively value access to the product or service.

That approach would make sense if you were only trying to estimate the value of the companies on the stock market. Stock prices reflect the expectation of the total present value of net revenue, extending out to the future. By that standard, Facebook and Twitter do in fact produce some value: Facebook had total revenues of $5.8 billion, and Twitter had revenues of $2.2 billion, in 2015. And their stock prices show optimism that will continue (Facebook's stock value exceeds $350 billion!).

But the value of Facebook and Twitter *to society* is the value enjoyed by the "commander" of the system, the consumer. How much value did consumers receive? If we try to measure that value, which economists call "consumer surplus," we have to look at the difference between *how much people would pay for access* to these platforms, and then subtract *the price they have to pay* (which is zero; Facebook and Twitter are free if you have a smartphone or computer and an internet connection.) How much would you pay to have access to Facebook? To Twitter? Perhaps $1 per year, if you do not like them much. Or $1,000 per year, or more, if you are a real fan. The point is that the amount that users *would* pay for these free services would vary, but the value they create is the consumer surplus, the extra value we get from having them available for free. In 2015 there were 1.6 billion registered Facebook users worldwide, and 310 million Twitter users.

Let's use the crudest possible measure: Let us just suppose that on average people would pay $12 per year for access to Facebook and $3 per year for access to Twitter. That's probably absurdly low, but we're just making up numbers here.

The value created by software, and social media platforms, derives from what people would pay, minus what they have to pay the provider. Facebook and Twitter create enormous value, but the way we measure output – called "GDP" by economists – only counts

Table 5.1 *Value of Social Media Platforms to Consumers*

Year 2015	Actual revenue	Users	Value created
Facebook	$5.8 billion	1.6 billion	$70 billion
Twitter	$2.2 billion	310 million	$1 billion
Totals	$8 billion	–	$71 billion

things that are actually sold, and then we only count them at the price at which they are sold.

There's your trouble, right there: GDP does not "count" free stuff. Many of the benefits of software platforms come from the enormous scale at which they can operate. Once a web site is operating (and assuming it has reasonable bandwidth in its connection), the marginal cost of an additional user, or an additional thousand users, is very nearly zero. If several million people visit Rotten Tomatoes, a movie review site, and get useful information about what film to go see, how do we value that? "We" do not; the only part of Rotten Tomatoes that "counts" toward GDP is their ad revenue. Information on the web wants to be *gratis*, not just *libre*.

This debate is now being carried out in a variety of circles, among economists such as Tyler Cowen and Brad DeLong, tech gurus such as Marc Andreessen, and journalists such as Tim Worstall (along with many others). We start with an empirical observation: the measured aspects of economic activity are slowing down, in some cases sharply, indicating a "stagnation" (in the words of Cowen, 2011). One possible explanation for this decrease is the enormous *increase in productivity* involved in substituting software for labor in a variety of service and information industries. That is, the stagnation is (mostly) real, but it may not be entirely or permanently bad.

A different explanation for the measured stagnation is the enormous *collapse in the prices* of services and information now available, dramatically increasing the amount and value of consumer surplus enjoyed by nearly everyone. That is, the stagnation is simply an artifact of the way we measure GDP – price times output, so that a huge output increase counts for nothing if the price is near zero – meaning that life is getting much, much better for most people and the problem is simply the way we measure economic activity. In this view, the stagnation is illusory. In fact, getting a lot of useful stuff for free is great for consumers and will drive the new economy. Not because workers want it, but because consumers do.

It is easy to see that both perspectives – increased productivity, or sharply reduced prices – can be correct and that these two views correspond to the two types of disruption we can expect. The reduction in prices, and the availability of an increasing variety of services and activities for free, or for a very low cost, is likely to provide a platform for leapfrogging the traditional stages of development and the usual institutions required for starting and running a business. This jumping will disrupt the banks, the courts, and the political entities that try to regulate and control business activities, but it will also allow people in nations that lack financial intermediaries, a system of law, and state capacity to provide infrastructure to become competitive. The "jump" type of disruption is *saltation*.

But there will also be problems. Those with access to a means of generating income can jump ahead; those left behind will suffer separation. Will the change be good or bad, overall? Perhaps the best summary is a "tweet," posted by Marc Andreessen (@pmarca on December 28, 2014): "Secular stagnation is an economist's Rorschach Test. It means different things to different people." Let's turn to saltation and separation.

Saltation: The "Virtue" of Backwardness

The word "saltation" is rarely used in conversation. It means an abrupt movement or transition, or (in evolutionary terms) a sudden discontinuous jump in a line of descent. The reason saltation is happening is that much of what we "know" about development, entrepreneurship, and the function of government and markets is based on certain assumptions about institutions and preconditions.[4] If a country is going to develop, it needs banks, rule of law, a judicial system that is not corrupt, a currency system, a road and rail system, access to ports, and so on. Or so says the conventional wisdom.

That same view – there are preconditions for development, and stages through which development takes place, stages that are nearly identical for all nations – is common in much of the scholarly work on development. This approach often follows Rostow (1960), who claimed that there were five essential – in fact, unavoidable – "stages of development":

(1) *Traditional society* (hierarchical, static, mostly agricultural)
(2) *Basic preconditions* (transition to manufacturing, development of trade infrastructure, and investment of profits in capital, not conspicuous consumption for the elite)
(3) *Take-off* (the destruction of traditional forms of production and professions, production turning to comparative advantage, developing division of labor)
(4) *Move toward maturity* (high levels of technology use in industry, sharp decline in population working in agriculture, professionalized private management and public service)
(5) *Mass consumption* (benefits of growth and development are widely shared, problems of income inequality and environment move to the fore because basic economic problems have been solved.)

Rostow saw this approach as being "anti-Communist," in the sense that it allows nations to develop without converting their political systems to central planning. But the approach is actually Marxist, in the sense that it is deterministic and materialist; it is just that Rostow thought capitalism was indefinitely sustainable.

One important response to the deterministic-materialist view is that of Gerschenkron (1962). Gerschenkron said:

---

[4] This essentially material, marginalist notion of "stages" of development is a central part of the theory of Karl Marx, who said "The country that is more developed industrially only shows, to the less developed, the image of its own future." (Marx, 1992, p. 13).

A good deal of our thinking about industrialization of backward countries is dominated – consciously or unconsciously – by the grand Marxian generalization according to which it is the history of advanced industrial countries [that is the future of developing countries] ... In some broad sense this generalization has validity ... But one should beware of accepting such a generalization too whole-heartedly ... In several very important respects the development of a backward country may, *by the very virtue of its backwardness*, tend to differ fundamentally from that of an advanced society.

(Gerschenkron, 1962, pp. 6–7; emphasis added)

Gerschenkron does not really mean that backwardness is a "virtue." It is not an advantage to lack the preconditions – banks, law, state capacity, infrastructure – of development. But in a world with Twitter, Ebay, Bitcoin, and Etherium, it is less of a disadvantage than ever before in human history. Even in the most remote places on earth, someone (let's call her "Parisa") can now rent a connection in an internet cafe, though the "cafe" may just be a tin-roofed shack with electricity supplied by a generator. Parisa can write code on an old desktop computer, with an old television-style monitor, and upload it to a "feature phone." Feature phones cannot run apps, but they can connect to the web at the "cafe."

It is important to understand this distinction because you may never have heard of a feature phone. In the developed world, we are used to "smart" phones, or pieces of hardware that have independent operating systems that are capable of running third-party software, or "apps," directly. A "feature phone," on the other hand, is a much cheaper, simpler piece of hardware (such as the LG "Extravert^{TM}" or the Samsung "Convoy^{TM}"). Parisa can buy a new one for less than $50; used and refurbished versions are available for $5 in many countries. Think about that: $5. For a connection to the world that will also display code, with a built-in hardware keyboard.

Combine Parisa's enhanced feature phone with a $1/hour for a web connection somewhere in town, or in a hut, and you are in business. There are more people now with wireless connections than with flush toilets, according to the United Nations (2013). Parisa can write apps and put them up for sale. Paradoxically, in fact, it is the writing of "apps" that makes feature phones so valuable: Parisa can write code and then store it and upload a new app, for sale for use by Android and iOS phones anywhere in the world, on a phone that itself will not run apps.[5] Or people who just conceive new apps for a living can subcontract the writing of the actual code to someone they have never met, based on their reputation on Linked-In and working the contract over Ethereum and being paid in bitcoin. You may not know what those things are because you live in a "developed" nation. But Parisa knows they are, and she uses them.

The tyranny of physical proximity and the need for functioning institutions is overthrown. Vigna and Casey (2015, pp. 1–3) tell the story of a real-life version of this young woman, Parisa Ahmadi, who graduated at the top of her class but who was relegated by custom and institutional capacity to house imprisonment in her family's home in Herat, Afghanistan. Parisa had no way to work, or to learn coding skills, or to pay for classes. But she used bitcoin to create an identity for herself, first as a student, and then as a producer of code and video content.

Because of the Internet, and Parisa's feature phone, competition for coding services and video content are global, truly global. A bid can be placed for a coding job, on a web site such as Freelancer.com, and within seconds it is visible to tens of millions of people like Parisa. The fact that there are no credit markets, or schools, or banks or attorneys in Herat once would have shut Parissa out. But now, because of

---

[5] Apple, Android, and a variety of other software providers have programs – Android Studio, Firebug, Dragonfly, Screencast, and Yslow – that will debug, for free, code written for their smart phones.

saltation, she can jump over all those obstacles and compete based on her own talents and initiative.

Separation

In Chapter 2, I talked about disruption, and the attempt by workers and industry to "sabotage" the machinery of change. But over and over we have seen that it is only possible to delay, not to prevent, economic revolutions.

The three most important effects of the Middleman/Sharing Revolution will be

(1) a reduction in the amount of physical stuff, in the form of consumer durables, being produced in factories by workers
(2) a decline in the cost of having access to a variety of stuff, and reduced needs for storage
(3) an ambiguous, but unsettling, effect on real wages, with both the direction and variance of real wages very much in flux

We tend to focus, in our own lives, on what economists call "nominal wages," or the money amount of our pay, the numbers printed on our paychecks. We are aware that the prices of the products that we buy affect the value of this paycheck, but mostly we think about how much we get paid.

Economists look at the aggregate effects of changes in prices as a predictor of the great movements in economic history, however. And we are entering a period where predictions are difficult, and the sense of risk that many people face is heightened. The reason is that the decline in manufacturing production will force nominal wages down. We are already seeing evidence of this in the world around us: The number of manufacturing jobs in the United States is changing rapidly. As Figure 5.1 shows, the relative size of the manufacturing sector has shrunk, in terms of proportion of the labor force, from 1 in 4 workers in 1970 to only around 1 in 10 workers in 2012.

Of course, decline in employment in one sector may be a good thing in terms of the dynamism of the economy. If the jobs are obsolete

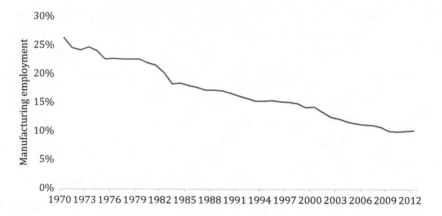

FIGURE 5.1 Manufacturing Employment as Proportion of Total U.S. Labor Force. Note: data series discontinued in 2012.

(remember the buggy whip manufacturers!), or if the decline in employment results from increased productivity, the move of labor to more socially useful employment is actually a benefit. It may not seem like a benefit to the worker who has to make the change, but the benefit to society is substantial. Consider Figure 5.2, which depicts the number of jobs, and the value of output, in manufacturing over time.

The number of manufacturing jobs has fallen dramatically, but there is no decline in the value of manufacturing output. In fact, when you consider that the price of many things – computers, televisions, and in some cases, adjusting for quality, cars – has *fallen*, the sustained increase in the value of manufacturing in the US economy is remarkable.

Figure 5.2 shows a prime cause of the second disruptive effect: *separation*. As there is less manufacturing on a broad scale, there has been far more "production" of value. An example is the iPad, which is "manufactured" outside of the United States. Still, consider this pie chart of value-added for the hardware and software components of the iPad.

If an iPad costs $600, this means that well over half of the new value it creates, $360, stays in the United States and is used to pay

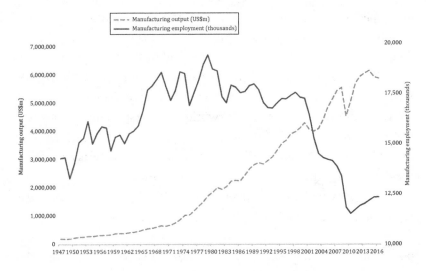

FIGURE 5.2 Manufacturing Output vs. Employment – 1947–2011

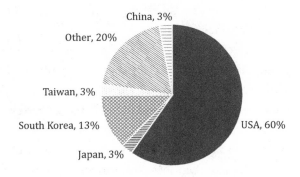

FIGURE 5.3 Distribution of Retail Value of iPad

designers, patent holders, and Apple as the company that licenses the iPhone brand. A number of other countries are paid for some components and assembly, but these are not very high wage jobs.

A small number of (mostly already wealthy) people in the United States make a lot of money by selling iPads, and Apple stockholders have made quite a bit of money from iPads. But very little of the manufacturing work is done in the United States. Small numbers of people with large wealth increases and large numbers of under-employed people implies *separation*: a permanent increase in the inequality of the distribution of wealth and income.

But separation in and of itself may not be unmanageable; in fact, it may not even be bad. It is true that the broadly shared distribution of wealth seen by much of the world – but especially the United States, in the period 1947 through 1983 – may be a thing of the past. But that broadly shared distribution was actually what was unusual in the first place. Much of the developed world was obliging enough to destroy its capital stock during World War II, and US labor was temporarily overvalued by historical standards.

So, we may just be returning to "normal," with permanent disparities in income. The difference in the Middleman/Sharing economy is that prices may fall far enough that the net effect, for many people, will be quite positive. When you consider the value – the consumer surplus[6] – available from a variety of activities that are essentially free for anyone with a smartphone, the decline in nominal wages may be less of a concern.

In fact, taking three factors together (a) the decline for the need for large houses, garages, closets, paid parking, kitchen counter space, and other storage; (b) the fact that products can be rented very cheaply if the density of transactions pushes down rental costs; and (c) free access to entertainment opportunities on social media, Keynes's two-day work week may be just around the corner. Marx's odd obsession with people defining themselves through their jobs was also an anomaly of a short period in history, the time since the start of the Industrial Revolution.

Before that, and perhaps again in the Middleman/Sharing economy, people may form identities around the groups they connect with. Before the Industrial Revolution, this meant a family, village, or region. Now, all sorts of new communities of meaning may be

---

[6] Remember that the "consumer surplus" is the difference between what consumers would pay and what price they are able to find in the market. The sum of total consumer surplus is the value created by a market economy. The market values of firms are derived from their ability to create consumer surplus.

formed by the groups we hang out with online. Status, identity, and satisfaction may derive from connections with people who are physically far, but virtually "close" in interest and shared passions.

There are signs of these changes already. "Games" such as World of Warcraft, Entropia, League of Legends, or Runescape have become communities, with tribes, alliances, and long-term relationships. I may work in a fast food restaurant, and live in my mother's basement, but online I wear the coveted "Helmet of Trials" and my stone is the "Symbol of Saradomin." The newbies all "friends chat" each other when my awesome avatar heaves into view, the object of respect and deference. Is this respect "fake"? Of course, but it is no more fake than the respect we give winners of "Survivor!", lottery winners with McMansions, or minor celebrities in many other settings. The point is that it is an identity.

You might object that it would somehow be better if we still all had manufacturing jobs, or at least if those jobs were available. I have to bring up James Taylor's song, "Millwork." The lyrics go like this:

> Millwork ain't easy, millwork ain't hard, millwork it ain't nothing but an awful boring job.
> I'm waiting for a daydream to take me through the morning and put me in my coffee break where I can have a sandwich and remember.
> Then it's me and my machine for the rest of the morning, for the rest of the afternoon and the rest of my life.

Millworkers in the American South were called "lintheads," and often died young of byssinosis, their lungs choked by cotton fibers (Christensen, 2010, p. 70). You can call those "good jobs" if you want to, but wearing the "Helmet of Trials" and beating the bejesus out of "Verac the Defiled" sounds like more fun.

More importantly, even if it is true that one might wish to live in high wage manufacturing days of the twentieth century, that's like asking why the hunter-gatherers moved to the cities. It is not a choice, but rather a consequence of a fundamental change in economic conditions. If prices fall far enough, it may be a viable identity to build a Range Tank account and smack down uppity Pures who are foolish enough to challenge you. (Sure, none of that makes any sense, unless you are in the Runescape community. But that's the point: There are many opportunities for exclusivity and status in a world where one can create one's own community.)

People are quite plastic mentally; we can adapt to the positional goods and definitions of status of almost any chosen community. Old people tend to want things: cars, houses, jewelry. Younger people – and you could see this on their Facebook pages, if any young people still used Facebook – are interested in experiences. Instead of saving for a 4,500 square foot McMansion, young people go to Madagascar or go hang gliding and then post the photos on Instagram. This trend is already taking the form of a dramatic decline in the proportion of young people who obtain driver's licenses: As recently as 1983, well over 90 percent of young people wanted to be able to drive a car. Now the proportion is only 75 percent and this number is falling fast.[7]

But even if people can do what they did for thousands of years before the Industrial Revolution and construct identities on a basis other than "jobs," there is another problem. That problem is that much of our ability to obtain income, retirement benefits, and health care is tied to "having a job." Can connection be broken? Can we move, as many people claim, into the "gig economy"?

GIGS: THE BOY WHO CRIED "ROBOT!"

In an article entitled, "A World Without Work," Derek Thompson (2015) tries to present a balance of perspectives:

> The job market defied doomsayers [who predicted "technological unemployment" after the Industrial Revolution], and according to the most frequently reported jobs numbers, it has so far done the

---

[7] Sivak and Schoettle (2016) and others who have interpreted their results have said "There is no obvious explanation" for these changes. I disagree. The answer is transactions costs.

same in our own time ... One could be forgiven for saying that recent predictions about technological job displacement are merely forming the latest chapter in a long story called *The Boys Who Cried Robot* – one in which the robot, unlike the wolf, never arrives in the end.

The end-of-work argument has often been dismissed as the "Luddite fallacy," an allusion to the nineteenth-century British brutes who smashed textile-making machines at the dawn of the industrial revolution, fearing the machines would put hand-weavers out of work ... What does the "end of work" mean, exactly? It does not mean the imminence of total unemployment, nor is the United States remotely likely to face, say, 30 or 50 percent unemployment within the next decade. Rather, technology could exert a slow but continual downward pressure on the value and availability of work – that is, on wages and on the share of prime-age workers with full-time jobs. Eventually, by degrees, that could create a new normal, where the expectation that work will be a central feature of adult life dissipates for a significant portion of society.

After 300 years of people crying wolf, there are now three broad reasons to take seriously the argument that the beast is at the door: the ongoing triumph of capital over labor, the quiet demise of the working man, and the impressive dexterity of information technology.

It is a central feature of the "software eats the world" view of the Middleman/Sharing revolution that capital (in the form of both machines and software) replaces workers but also makes the workers who remain much more productive. But do we really expect "the demise of the working man"? Or will the nature of work shift, as it has in the past?

The idea of a "gig economy" is old, but the possibilities for serial short-term employment, or "gigs" are expanding rapidly.[8] It will not surprise the reader to learn that the reason is that entrepreneurs have

---

[8] The word "gig" itself apparently dates to the thirteenth century, and variously meant a "giddy girl," a "spinning, bouncing top," or later a light, bouncy carriage. The original use of the word in the sense of a short-term job, is apparently in the music

found ways to sell reductions in transaction costs. Self-employed people – plumbers, electricians, and carpet cleaners, for example, have long worked "gigs": They schedule calls to some location where they go and do their work, according to the instructions of the customer, and then get paid and perhaps not see that customer again.

But that has not been the practice in many kinds of work and production. The reason is transaction costs, of course. As Coase (1937) pointed out, it is cheaper (in terms of recontracting and negotiating deals) to have *employees* who can be assigned tasks on an ad hoc basis than it is to *hire people for gigs* on an ad hoc basis. But this is just the "rent vs. own" decision again, except in labor markets. If the costs of renting a worker for just a few hours are low enough, there is little reason for employers to commit to long-term contracts. In traditional jobs, employers must buy all the employees' work time for years and then try to figure out how to keep them busy. Consequently, it is becoming more common for firms to "rent" workers instead of taking on full-time employees.

This has had a striking implication in terms of what we might think of as a "firm." Most *workers* still work for large firm – what Cowen and Parker (1997) call "Sloan Firms," after Alfred P. Sloan's conception of the business enterprise. But if you think of the legal and contractual "person" of all incorporated firms as the units of analysis, the average number of employees has fallen by about 25 percent (Wright, 2013, using Bureau of Labor Statistics data). Further, most "new" firms, on net, have been the incorporation of an individual for the purposes of working gigs. Consider Figure 5.4.

As you can see, there are 10 million new "firms" with no employees, a 60 percent increase. The number of firms with at least one employee, however, has remained flat for the last twenty years.

---

industry, especially the jazz or blues genre of music. But later gig came to mean any short-term, even one-off, employment with no benefits and no guarantee of a return engagement.

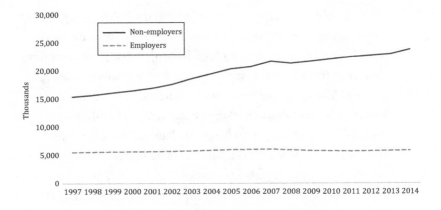

FIGURE 5.4 Almost All New Firms Are "non-employers"

In terms of proportions, that means that more than 80 percent of all firms have no traditional employees.

Thus, there are two divergent trends, which seem contradictory. More workers now work for (a few) large firms, but most firms have very few many fewer employees. Workers who once would have been called "temps" are now contractors, working in the gig economy. If this movement continues, the very notion of a "firm" may be blurred. A group of people, each with specialized skills and a ratings-based reputation on Linked-In, would be hired for a project. At the project's completion, the group would break up, only to reform anew in kaleidoscopically different combinations of workers and projects.

Hollywood films, for example, were once made by the major "studios" such as Metro-Goldwyn-Mayer or twentieth-century Fox. These firms now are distributors, and movies are made by "gig" workers, hired for the duration of the shooting of the film. After the film is completed, the gig is over. Adam Davidson (2015) describes "Hollywood Model" of gig employment like this:

> Recently I visited a movie set. It was the first day of production, and
> I arrived just as the sun was coming up, but already, around
> 150 people were busy setting up that day's shot in an abandoned
> office building. Crew members were laying electric cables and

hanging lights ... Carpenters were putting the finishing touches on a convincing prop elevator – I pushed the call button and waited, until I finally realized it was a fake. [I tried] to figure out something that mystified me as the day went on: Why was this process so smooth? The team had never worked together before, and the scenes they were shooting that day required many different complex tasks to happen in harmony: lighting, makeup, hair, costumes, sets, props, acting. And yet there was no transition time; everybody worked together seamlessly, instantly. The set designer told me about the shade of off-white that he chose for the walls, how it supported the feel of the scene. The costume designer had agonized over precisely which sandals the lead actor should wear. They told me all this, but they didn't need to tell one another. They just got to work, and somehow it all fit together.

... A project is identified; a team is assembled; it works together for precisely as long as is needed to complete the task; then the team disbands. This short-term, project-based business structure is an alternative to the corporate model, in which capital is spent up front to build a business, which then hires workers for long-term, open-ended jobs that can last for years, even a lifetime.

In a way, none of this is surprising: Specialization and the gains from division of labor are limited by the extent of the cooperation horizon. If the transaction costs of extreme specialization can be reduced, the scope for innovation is expanded. Hollywood has full-time professional "bug wranglers" to manage scenes with bugs as "actors."[9] No studio might be able to afford a full-time bug wrangler, so under the old system the job did not exist. But in the gig economy, with a thousand films all being made simultaneously by an ephemeral but highly organized team of the sort Adam Davidson describes, there may be enough work to keep several bug wranglers busy full time, in a city as large as Los Angeles or Mumbai.

---

[9] Yes, really, people do that, though they probably do not use their job as a pick-up line in singles bars.

There are some clear advantages to the gig economy, for both workers who have specialized skills and for companies trying to remain small and nimble.

> The changing needs of today's workers, the war for talent and the globalization of the workforce are just a few reasons that today's technology is evolving so rapidly. All of these forces are driving workforce management to the top of the business agenda, especially as talent becomes a true differentiator for organizations. ... It affords companies access to pre-screened, pre-trained workers with niche skills, who can get to work quickly and stay on only for as long as they are needed. And, as a company's needs change, an external workforce can be scaled up or down quickly.
>
> *(Arun Srinivasan, quoted in White, 2016)*

Coase said that firms only exist if they are lower transaction costs means of organizing production. But that formulation is consistent with the existence of "firms" that have exactly one employee, who is also the CEO. Firms may be able to rent capital equipment and labor for very short periods, increasing the productivity of the workers for the period that they are employed and dramatically reducing the fixed costs of the firm. In the limit, firms themselves might simply become small teams that hire out for specific projects. Workers in this system would be private contractors, not "employees" in the traditional sense. Unsurprisingly, the counter-revolutionary fervor of those who wish to protect existing power structures of both firms and unions will call for attempts to control the sale of transaction cost reductions.

In the next and final chapter, I will take up some broader issues, raised by the changes the Middleman/Sharing revolution will force on our economy and our society. Something has got to give.

6   The Day after Tomorrow

There is a long history of businesses that try to deprive workers of the protections and benefits they are entitled to under the law by wrongly treating them as independent contractors, rather than employees. Now, some workers and regulators are accusing companies like Uber, which connects cars with passengers on mobile apps, of doing the same thing to the thousands of drivers, couriers and others who work for them.

Agricultural businesses, textile mills, construction firms and other enterprises have often classified workers as contractors to lower their costs ... In recent years, app-based businesses like Uber, Lyft and Instacart have grown rapidly, in part because they signed up tens of thousands of people to work on their services as independent contractors. Uber, the most successful business in this sector, has signed up more than 160,000 of what it calls "driver-partners." There is no question that the companies in what some people call the "gig economy" would not have been able to grow so fast if they had hired all of these people as employees.

"Defining 'Employee' in the Gig Economy," *New York Times*

Looking back, the Industrial Revolution appears to have been inevitable. Looking back at the Neolithic revolution, it is hard to pierce through the mental construct of "society" based in cities that we now take for granted and imagine the world of hunter-gatherer clans.

I imagine that something very like that retrospective incomprehension will be the reaction of people just fifty years from now, when they learn that we had expensive cars that mostly sat still in garages and parking lots, and that we had houses and closets full of things we rarely used. They will also find it hard to imagine that, in the United States at least, only the people who had jobs could obtain health care but that jobs themselves were hard to obtain. They will compare the fact that many people in the twentieth century worked their entire careers for one company to the practice of "villeinage" in medieval England, where serfs were tied to the land and could not move around without their master's permission.

Obviously, much of the book so far has been speculative, though the speculation has been based on thinking pretty hard about the implications and application of economic principles. But in this chapter, I am going to abandon modesty completely, and speculate more broadly, about the day *after* Tomorrow 3.0.

THE WAY THINGS HAVE ALWAYS BEEN

There have always been questions about "where will the jobs come from?" The capitalist system does not produce jobs; it produces consumer surplus. Consumers direct capital, through the intervention and agency of entrepreneurs, toward the uses that consumers subjectively value. Entrepreneurs make profits, and workers are paid wages, only to the extent that their activities produce value for consumers.

But we want the economy to do more; we *want* the economy to "produce jobs." The problem is that capitalism is animated by a constant search for profits, which (in competitive industries) turns into a drive to cut costs. Since all firms cut costs, and in mostly the same ways, this means that prices to consumer fall. But workers find that there are fewer jobs as costs are cut and labor is replaced by capital in the form of tools or automation, and so on.

There's a story of an economist visiting an Asian country. He was proudly shown a huge, busy work site where thousands of workers were beavering away constructing a dam. Most of the work was being done with shovels and wheelbarrows. The economist asked why there were so few bulldozers or trucks. One of the hosts explained that they were trying to create jobs, to help the economy. The economist said, "Oh, I'm sorry. I misunderstood. I thought you were producing a dam. If you are trying to produce *jobs*, you should take away all those shovels and wheelbarrows and give the workers sticks and clay bowls."

The history of economic growth and development is tale of displacement and chaos. As people figured out ways to expand the cooperation horizon, first in cities using specialization, the result has been consistent replacement of inefficient production processes by new and better ways of making things. One hundred thousand people with sticks could build a small dam, but it would take a while. One thousand people with shovels and wheelbarrows could build a better dam, and faster, than a hundred thousand with sticks. But one hundred highly skilled workers with modern bulldozers and trucks could build an enormous dam quite quickly.

Of course, small communities do not need enormous dams. So they do not need heavy equipment, or skilled operators. The infrastructure that supports cooperation at scale is never developed, without the force of economic change expanding the cooperation horizon. But when the scale of specialization, particularly division of labor, is expanded by market forces, the option of one hundred workers with advanced machines becomes available. Nine hundred workers who once had reliable paychecks using shovels and wheelbarrows are out of a job. They were good at using shovels and wheelbarrows, but they cannot drive a bulldozer. And they certainly cannot write computer programs in Python or create usable HTML code.

Add this to the workers displaced from furniture factories, textiles, automobiles, steel, and a thousand other activities. What happens when the logic of cost reduction, now in the form of the Middleman-Sharing economy, displaces thousands of workers? One possibility we have already talked about: violence, sabotage, and politically popular regulations to slow the pace of change and protect jobs. But that's hardly a solution, and in fact it makes the problem worse in some ways. If we create artificial incentives to retain obsolete economic institutions and forms of production, we are actually giving people a signal that they should obtain training, and experience, in industries that are still going to disappear. Delaying that disappearance for five or ten years and robbing people of the chance to get more useful education and experience during their twenties and thirties is a trap; it's not the solution.

The logic of labor markets is based on price, especially a specific price called "wages." Unemployment can result if wages are too high; to put it another way, if wages fall far enough, then it will be worth hiring more workers. But societies may not be able, or politically willing, to rely on adjustments in wages to "solve" problems of unemployment. The fact that there is some positive wage where workers displaced by the dynamics of "creative destruction" can find jobs is poor comfort if that wage is so low that they cannot make a living. Even if one grants that unemployment is in some sense "voluntary," because one can always find a job at *some* wage, the disruption of losing a factory job that paid $55,000 per year and taking a job that pays $11,000 a year is wrenching.

Recent policy solutions may actually be part of the problem. The urge to ensure a "living wage" is understandable as an ethical impulse, if the rate of increase of wages seems insufficient to help the lowest-income group of citizens to live in society. The problem is that there is little reason to expect minimum wages to provide a living wage, because wages are a price that measures particular kinds of scarcity, at the margin of the labor market. A recent study from the National Bureau of Economic Research (Jardim et al., 2017) estimated that the Seattle, Washington labor market showed a decline in hours worked for the poorest workers. The fall in hours more than offset the increased pay per hour, meaning that the workers lost income as a result of increasing the minimum wage to $13. The increase to $15 may have even sharper damaging effects.

It's not hard to see how this might happen. When you go into a fast food restaurant, you look up on the menu board, and then you read some words: "Two hamburgers, fries, and a drink" or "frozen yogurt with sprinkle topping." The person behind the counter looks for the corresponding words on his or her cash register, and then reads the price that the machine computes. You hand the person some money, and he or she makes change.

At a wage of $8, that might continue. But if the wage goes up – and especially if it almost doubles, to $15 – things change. All management has to do is to *turn the cash register around*. Instead of *saying* the words and having the worker press the "hamburger," "fries," and "drink" buttons, the customer can do it. Instead of handing the worker payment, the customer can push cash or a chipped credit card into a slot. Using a few tweaks to the existing hardware of cash registers, software can be written that eats the world of service jobs.

Of course, the cost savings are even bigger if more skilled services can be replaced by software. Simplecontacts.com administers eye exams and gives vision prescriptions using your smart phone. Easydiagnosis.com is an expert system for collecting and interpreting basic medical examination and lab results. The software doesn't miss anything, it doesn't get tired, and it doesn't have hunches that persist in the face of contrary evidence.[1]

The final problem with the Middleman/Sharing Revolutions, is that "this time" may be different. Until now we have relied on a dynamic economy driven by new consumption as a motor for job growth. Yes, entrepreneurs make new products, things that consumers want and for which they will pay a premium. And that wipes out old products.

Those workers have always found jobs making the new products. But what if the "new products" are software, which wants to be free? The prices of access to many "products," including Facebook, Google, and Twitter, are all essentially zero. And the economies of scale in "production" are so large that even these companies have relatively few employees. Facebook had only 2,500 employees as recently as 2010, and still employs fewer than 25,000. For the sake of comparison, General Motors had more than 350,000 employees just thirty years ago.

In Chapter 5, I discussed two very different kinds of disruption, saltation and separation. *Saltation* can benefit displaced workers because it means that there are new industries that need workers, and people who can quickly acquire new skills and "jump" will be able to command a premium. *Separation* is not so good. Separation means that for many people – who have lost a job for which they had

---

[1] For a much more nuanced view, with some of the history of medical expert systems, see Mukherjee (2017). It may be that the either/or distinction is misleading. Trained humans using the results provided by better software may both improve outcomes, reduce costs, and at the same time produce more jobs.

trained and had skills – there is no easy way to pay for the education and experience that would be required to take advantage of saltation.

The paradox is that capital (and that includes software) destroys jobs but makes jobs that adapt and survive much more productive. Economists describe the process of wage determination in an economy as resting on the worker's "value of marginal product," or VMP.

Value of Marginal Product = Price of Output
× Marginal Amount of Output

VMP is the result of multiplying the price of the output times the "marginal" or incremental amount of the product that the worker adds to output. Capital makes workers *much* more productive; that's why the bulldozer operator makes far more than the guy with a shovel who makes more than a guy with a stick.

Software can work the same way, but with a twist. We tend to think of workplace dynamics in a kind of "us vs. them" way, with a romantic contest between man and machine. But for the most part that's wrong: Machines – including software – make workers more productive. To take a whimsical example, there was an audible gasp around the world when the IBM computer, "Deep Blue," defeated chess grandmaster Garry Kasparov in 1997. Oh, no, computers are going to take over!

In fact, that's a misunderstanding. It is still true that a team of an expert human and a computer, with highly specialized software adapted to the task at hand, can rather easily defeat either (a) a human, or (b) a machine. The point is that it is people using machines that is the powerful combination. The worker with a power loom was more powerful, in economic terms, than the worker with a hand loom, who in turn was able to make better clothing than someone who sewed animal skins, with a bone needle.

So, perhaps we can work around the enormous increase in productivity that will result from pairing workers with specialized machines and software (Bessen, 2015; Mindell, 2015). But how can we work around the fact that the price of output is going to fall dramatically? If the VMP is the *product* of output price and productivity, falling output price means wages must fall, unless productivity can increase by more than output price falls.

It has been the argument of this book that there are two complementary but distinct forces that will cause prices to plummet. The first is the expanding middleman economy, where software innovations shared as "apps" on smartphones, connected over the Internet, will drive down prices as entrepreneurs are increasingly able to sell reductions in transaction costs. The second is the sharing economy, which has barely begun to be noticeable, where rental and sharing arrangements replace inefficient and clumsy mechanisms of exclusive ownership.

The combination will bring prices down, sharply. And the inventory of each of the products that will be needed will decline, also. At first, as the composition of the stock of durables is transformed from "short-lived and quickly broken" to "commercial grade and long-lived" there will be a short burst of production increases. But once we have made millions of durable, rugged power drills and espresso machines and other rentable items, the market for production will stagnate even further: not only will we need less, but each one we do make will last longer because it is made to be rented by the thousands, not be owned by one person who rarely uses it.

The "rent v. own" decision will also extend to a variety of other items, including some that we think of now as being quite personal. There are more than 250 new companies specializing in clothing rentals, including designer fashion that have until now been quite out of the reach of most consumers. The best known may be "Rent the Runway," which rents haute couture, but the levels of price and quality vary substantially. The point is that you may not need a closet in your home if you can have what entrepreneurs are calling "your closet in the cloud."

Rent the Runway – founded in 2010 and now attracting more than $100 million per year in revenues – has a subscription service it calls the "Unlimited." For $139 per month the customer can have three items at a time; shipping is paid for by the company. That means that you can have a "new" coat-dress-handbag combination, or skirt-blouse-blazer ensemble, every month, or *every week* if you want. As Brooke Hartmann, subscription director, puts it: "Imagine your closet has a trapdoor in the back and it opens to the Rent the Runway warehouse." (Willett, 2016). And while Rent the Runway is the largest and best known of these new companies, that could change quickly. Companies such as Chic by Choice, The Black Tux, Borrowing Magnolia Mine, or Le Tote are all looking for new niches and new ways to create a closet in the cloud.

There are likely new things being shared by renting that I have not listed, and some of the companies I have discussed may have gone out of business by the time you read this. The fact is that I do not know which items or products are "worth" renting; we are facing a period of trial and error. It is important to stay focused on the larger picture: I'm not making a specific claim about any one product. What I'm saying is that in a world where entrepreneurs can commodify (a) reductions in transaction costs and (b) excess capacity, the likely disruptions in traditional ways of doing business will be both significant and very hard to foresee.

As Gates Saterfield, a "visionist" (really) at the American Sartorial Institute put it in an interview with the *Wall Street Journal's* Joe Queenan:

> If you're self-employed and do not have to go to an office every day, you do not really need to own your own pants. You might need a pair of pants a few hours a week. So it is not hard to imagine a situation where groups of men pool their resources to share pants on a need-to-wear basis. The same goes for quality men's footwear.

Maybe it is because I'm not a "visionist," but that scenario is a *little* hard to imagine. To be fair, we are not talking about jeans or even chinos here but about high quality "business casual" dress pants. The dress code in Silicon Valley and many of the most productive sectors of the new economy is pretty loose. If you had an app that could give accurate laser measurements of your proportions, you could have high quality clothing delivered, and returned, all in the same day, without taking up closet space. Maybe it is not so visionary after all.

About ten years ago, I made a prediction along these lines, regarding employees, in my "Bosses Don't Wear Bunny Slippers":

> So, one day the boss has this crazy thought. He asks himself a question that has never occurred to him before: Why have any employees at all? Why have a building? Why not just sit home, wearing his jammies and bunny slippers, sipping a nice cup of tea, and outsource everything? He can write contracts to buy parts, he can pay workers to assemble the parts, and he can use shipping companies to box and transport the product.
>
> The boss is elated. He never really liked these people anyway. Always asking questions, constantly looking for direction and expecting him to know the answers. He fires all his employees, effective one month from now, and takes bids on all the design, parts manufacture, assembly, and shipping that those people used to do.
>
> (Munger, 2008)

In other words, the three apparently very different decisions (hire vs. contract out, make vs. buy, and rent vs. own) are all surprisingly similar. The correct decision is variable and highly contingent, and the contingency depends on transaction costs.

What is clear is that the net effect, for many people, will be neutral or even positive. Their nominal wages (the number on their paycheck) will fall. On the other hand, the prices of many products will fall by even more, and lots of things will be free. As that process plays out, it is hard to predict the effects of lower prices because in a dynamic economy people will have more money to spend on other things. We may all want much more of the services that are now cheaper.

One famous example is the technology we now call "ATMs" or Automatic Teller Machines. At first, people were worried that software would eat the world of branch banking and that all the human tellers would lose their job. But a surprising thing happened: Since many of the mundane transactions were handled so cheaply by software on the ATM, it became possible to open more actual branches. Remember, the number of human tellers employed at local branches went up, not down, after the introduction of ATMs. As I said, it is hard to predict.

THE DIFFERENCE BETWEEN "LESS JOB" AND "NO JOB"

For some people at least, the problem won't be "less job"; for many people who now work in jobs they hate, having "less job" will be just fine. The real problem will be "no job." And the gig economy is only a partial answer. On the popular podcast, *EconTalk*, hosted by Russ Roberts, a guest made the following observation about automation and job loss.

> Always with automation it is always easier to see the jobs that get lost than the ones that are going to get created. Because, you know, things will become cheaper, so there will be a demand for complementary goods; people will just have more disposable income that they will use to buy other things. There will be whole new categories of jobs that are created. In the nineteenth century, most Americans were farmers; and then all those jobs disappeared. But it is not like 95 percent of Americans aren't employed. They are just doing things that were unimaginable back then, like "app designer."
>
> ... But let's imagine ... if there is a future where robots and computers can do everything better than people. What will happen then? ... It's one thing with an unemployment rate of 5 percent. Once the unemployment rate reaches 50 percent, everybody is going to vote for very generous unemployment benefits–or for redistributing the wealth. In a democracy, everybody has a vote.
>
> ... And people are already talking things like having a *universal basic income*. It's of course a controversial topic. But I, for one, think that even today it would already be better today to have something like that than to have something like the patchwork of all these different things that, many of them are very inefficient,

subject to capture by different special interest groups. We would be better to have a simpler, more uniform solution. And then what the level of that basic income is, well, that can change, depending on the progress of technology, depending on the economic conditions, and the politics and so forth.

(Domingos, 2016; emphasis added)

There are two reasons why this suggestion of a "basic income," or floor on the level of economic abjectness, seems like a badly flawed but possibly workable solution. The first is that we are tempted to ask whether the Middleman/Sharing revolution is "good" or "bad." But that simplistic dichotomy is misleading; it will be both. Overall, there will be many benefits, and the general condition of humanity will improve, as we make more efficient – and less environmentally damaging – the use of the resources we already have. But it is just not true that "everyone" will be better off. Many people who played by the rules and took jobs that required specific training are going to be stuck. Some people worry that the coming revolution will make inequality of income and wealth much worse, while others see software as producing an egalitarian utopia. I think the answer is that both things will happen at the same time, and often to the same people.

Second, the Middleman/Sharing Revolution is inevitable: It's going to happen, and it is not a choice. Even those who are in some ways better off may feel exposed to risk of economic displacement. So while one might not grant that some form of "social insurance" is morally justified, it might be politically expedient.

Would a "universal basic income" be an answer? It would be only be an imperfect, and partial, answer of course. But the policy question is whether some social response is morally necessary and politically inevitable. If the answer is "yes," then let's consider whether a universal basic income is a good start.

A common objection is that a basic income guarantee (BIG) just "pays people not to work." But that's not quite right. *Current* welfare programs do that: If you find a job, you lose your benefits. As it stands, public assistance policy traps people by imposing an effective marginal tax rate of 50 percent or higher: If I get a job making $20,000 a year, I lose $10,000 in benefits, so I'm only "making" an extra $10,000 by working, and I have to pay for transportation and child care in after-tax dollars. It is the *current* system that forces people not to work because of what economists call a "price effect": the net benefit to working is so small I'm better off staying home.

A BIG would pay everyone, even if they have a job.[2] Of course, we would have to implement an exchange:

(1) The state and federal governments will scrap a long list of existing programs (purportedly) designed to equalize income or to provide a safety net for the least well-off. Everything. That includes minimum wage laws, Social Security, and all forms of housing subsidies and wage regulations must go. And never come back. If a constitutional amendment is required to enforce this commitment, fair enough.

(2) In exchange, and in a once-and-for-all replacement, a comprehensive BIG would be implemented as a single cash-payment replacement.

There are two common objections.

First, "That could never actually happen."

The second is "Choice? You think we want to give people choices? They can't *handle* choices!"

But the BIG proposal cannot be blamed just because it would not be implemented. I recognize that it will be difficult to give up the whole dog's breakfast of different programs that elites and political officials now use to claim credit and buy votes. It may be true that BIG would be on top of, rather than instead of, existing programs. But then that's not the proposal being considered. Making the argument that politicians will not implement the proposal is the sort of thing you might hear in a high school debate class: Since you cannot win on the merits, change the question.

---

[2] An interesting proposal, along the lines of "Uber, but for _____," is "Uber, but for welfare" (Warstler, 2014; Conda and Khanna, 2016).

The second objection – people cannot be trusted to make their own choices – is even worse. That's simply inconsistent with democracy. It may be true that if we give people choices some will make bad ones. But increasing poor peoples' capacity will mean that they have choices *to make*, and some of them –perhaps many – will recognize that for the first time they are being entrusted with responsibility.

It is an old problem: Should we give poor people an in-kind transfer (say, vouchers for food or housing)? Or should we give people an amount of money equal to the *cost* of that in-kind transfer? Given the fungibility of money, the recipients of the cash have to be at least as well-off as the recipients of the food, since the first group could always buy the food if that is what is best for them. But they could also buy *something else*, if that is what is better, *for them*. The enormous variety of in-kind programs and vouchers are costly precisely because they are all an attempt to force poor people to make "good" (in the eyes of voters or bureaucrats) choices. Not surprisingly, some food stamps and other in-kind vouchers are then sold on the black market at a substantial discount.[3]

IF A BIG IS THE ANSWER, WHAT IS THE QUESTION?

The problem that the world economy must deal with, and that public policy must squarely address, is this: two very different trends are pushing us in opposite directions. The first trend is a rapid movement toward cheaper, better, more flexible services available through software on portable platforms. The second trend is a sharp, and accelerating, disparity in annual income and total wealth. The new economy is likely to make this worse, possibly much worse.

The first trend is (almost) all positive. There was a famous "meme" that circulated on Facebook in 2014, showing an image of a

---

[3] While the amounts of fraud have at some points been substantial, it appears that the current use of EBT cards requiring an ID have reduced the total proportion of fraudulent spending below 3 percent of the total amount paid out. See, for a history, Rude (2017). Thus, while fraud exists, it would likely exist under a BIG program as well.

full-page 1991-era ad for Radio Shack, an electronics store (Cichon, 2014). The ad listed more than a dozen different products, ranging from fax machines to word processors to cassette players to cameras and camcorders. The meme had this text at the bottom of the image: "Today all this is one smart phone."

The total cost of all the various items was well in excess of $3,000, and that's in 1994 dollars. That stuff, if it were available, would cost more than $5,000. But a lot of it is not available because nobody wants a hand calculator or a VCR camcorder instead of a smart phone. You could spend $5,000 on a smart phone, of course – the Tonino Lamborghini 88 Tauri is listed at $5,250. But a standard iPhone or Galaxy can be had for 10 percent of that price, and it will do all those things better than each of the separate gadgets in 1991. And it will fit comfortably in your pocket. Adjusting for cost reduction and quality improvement, in other words, that's a 1000 percent improvement.

The reason this is important is that it levels people, or at least people in advanced societies. As John Nye points out (Nye, 2017):

> Today while I was out running errands in my 5-year-old Honda Accord, I passed a Tesla ... In practical terms, the difference between a $200,000 Tesla and my last car, a beat-up minivan worth $2,000 at trade-in, is not all that large. They're both safe forms of transportation that get you from point A to point B and, given legal limits and the reality of suburban traffic, most of the time they're driven at roughly the same speeds.
>
> In that sense, measures of income inequality overstate the differences within a developed country like the United States. The products available to the masses are, in many cases, nearly as good as those available only to the elite. Your garbageman's old Timex and your podiatrist's brand new Rolex serve almost precisely the same function.

So, while there's a difference between a black plastic digital watch and a fully iced-up platinum watch, the functional difference is negligible. In fact, the digital watch may even keep better time than the heavy, expensive analog version. The expensive watch has higher social status, but that's something that is socially constructed rather than something necessary to tell time.

Overall, the biggest differences between a middle-class person and an upper class person is the size of their houses and age of their scotch. They probably both have 50-inch flat screen 4k televisions, if they want them. In practical terms, the universal availability of products is reducing differences based on income, and the changes in the "new" economy will accelerate that leveling. We need to enable those changes to work their magic.

The second trend is more troubling because it cuts the other way. It is all very well to say that there are few practical differences in quality of life, but the degree of inequality itself raises questions about the basic fairness of the system. Further, even if the middle and lower class on average are in improved circumstances there is a widely shared perception that everyone thinks they are losing. The "losing" may take the form of falling behind, but it is also a sense of insecurity because the current levels of income are endangered by rapid and unpredictable changes in the economy.

Worse, to the extent that effective access to digital technology is crucial for connecting to job opportunities and the leveling effects of powerful devices, there are substantial differences across income groups. According to work reported on by Anderson (2017), almost half of the poorest third of Americans have access to home wifi connections and laptop or desktop computers. Nearly 2/3 of this group do have cell phones, but 5G connections are an expensive way to buy data and many poor people scrimp on those phone capabilities as a result. Further, more than 60 percent of the poorest Americans rarely or never use the Internet as part of their jobs, reducing their familiarity with the fast-changing tools and apps that are available.

What would a BIG program do to address this problem? It won't solve it, but it might limit the political and social problems we face while improving on the efficiency of current programs.

BACKGROUND AND DEFINITIONS

- A BIG program is a negative head tax, a lump sum payment simply for being alive. There is no means test, or work requirement. This means that it has all the "good" properties – in terms of efficiency and absence of distortion – of any head tax.[4]
- A Negative Income Tax (NIT) program is one means of implementing a BIG. I am proposing to pick a NIT to implement a BIG. The infrastructure, in the form of the US Treasury Department and its tax collection agency the Internal Revenue Service is already set up to perform these functions, and so little new bureaucracy or rule-making would be required.

The origins of what we now think of as a BIG are obscure. One clear antecedent is in the French Republican tradition, especially Thomas Paine drawing on Rousseau's idea of property. A "solution" that a number of people settled on was some form of compensation for resource use. For some, the focus was narrowly on land as the key resource, requiring a tax on land rent (George, 1951). More interesting, for purposes of situating the BIG historically, is Thomas Paine's 1795 "Agrarian Justice" pamphlet, in which he advocated not just a tax on land, but the use of that revenue to fund a universal "ground rent" payment.

> [T]he earth, in its natural, cultivated state was, and ever would have continued to be, the common property of the human race ... But the earth in its natural state, as before said, is capable of supporting but a small number of inhabitants compared with what it is capable of doing in a cultivated state. And as it is impossible to separate the improvement made by cultivation from the earth itself, upon which that improvement is made, the idea of landed property arose from that parable connection; but it is nevertheless true, that *it is the value of the improvement, only, and not the earth itself, that is individual property.*

---

[4] Lump sum or "head" taxes are the least distortive of all taxes, precisely because their amount is fixed and does not change in response economic station or work effort. See, for a review, Graaf (1987, pp. 251–252), and Munger (2015b).

Every proprietor, therefore, of cultivated lands, owes to the community a ground-rent (for I know of no better term to express the idea) for the land which he holds; and it is from this ground-rent that the fund proposed in this plan is to issue.

... [I propose] to create a national fund, out of which there *shall be paid to every person, when arrived at the age of twenty-one years, the sum of fifteen pounds sterling, as a compensation in part, for the loss of his or her natural inheritance,* by the introduction of the system of landed property:

And also, the sum of *ten pounds per annum, during life, to every person now living,* of the age of fifty years, and to all others as they shall arrive at that age.

(Paine, 1795, emphasis added)

Paine seems to be arguing that the "ground rent" can serve as the sole revenue source for a universal BIG. That claim can certainly be criticized, on either equity grounds or empirical validity. But there are examples of this sort of logic at work. The US state of Alaska established in 1980 the "Alaska Permanent Fund," with a constitutional amendment that required that "At least 25 percent of all mineral lease rentals, royalties, royalty sales proceeds, federal mineral revenue-sharing payments and bonuses received by the state be placed in a permanent fund, the principal of which may only be used for income-producing investments." (Alaska Permanent Fund, n.d.) The income derived from the endowment created out of the depletion of natural resources in Alaska is divided up among all permanent citizens of Alaska, with some restrictions for access and residency. As Widerquist and Howard (2012) have noted, the Alaska experience might provide a model that shows how payments might work and how they might be financed.

WHY ARE THERE POOR PEOPLE?

There's a more potent, and empirical, argument for a BIG. It is quite simple: Given how much we spend on poverty, there *cannot* be any poor people in the United States. If we take the total amount spent on poverty programs, and divide it by the number of people in poverty, the income per capita is above the poverty line. Problem solved.

But the money is not reaching the poor. Tanner (2012) sums it up this way:

> [T]his year the federal government will spend more than $668 billion on at least 126 different programs to fight poverty. And that does not even begin to count welfare spending by state and local governments, which adds $284 billion to that figure. In total, the United States spends nearly $1 trillion every year to fight poverty. That amounts to $20,610 for every poor person in America, or $61,830 per poor family of three.

If they were actually receiving the money, that $61,000 would put a family of three above not just above the poverty line but above *average* income for the population. What gives?

Well, we do. Taxpayers. Poor people aren't receiving the money, but we are definitely giving it. The money gets diverted into administration, spent on in-kind rather than direct assistance, and used to fund expensive meetings where smart people sit and worry about what to do about poverty.

To be fair, Tanner's estimate of "poverty" programs includes a substantial component that are health care subsidies, with the largest being Medicaid ($228 billion per year). Adjusting his figures to remove the health care portion reduces total expenditures to about $700 billion per year, for a population of 50 million "poor" Americans, gives a figure of about $14,000 per person in spending. For a family of three, this would be $42,000 per year, more than the poverty rate (Dept. of Health and Human Services, 2014) of about $20,000 but less than the average family income.

In other ways, Tanner's figure is a substantial *underestimate* because he is focusing on transfers. But there are other programs, programs whose costs are hard to estimate, that are also designed to help the poor. Two important examples are minimum wage laws and mass transit systems. Measuring the effects of minimum wage laws is difficult. But the combination of a high minimum wage law and unemployment compensation that is contingent on the recipient remaining unemployed act as a devastating one-two punch on the young people growing up in urban poor families.

The effect is far less significant for white or middle-class young people, according to the Bureau of Labor Statistics (BLS, 2014). In July 2014, the overall youth unemployment rate was 14.3 percent (though with a participation rate of only 58 percent, there are many young people who are not even looking for work, and so are not "unemployed"). For black males, however, this unemployment rate is more than 25 percent, meaning that for fully one-quarter of those young men actively looking for work there is no job to be had. Getting rid of the minimum wage would open up more jobs to those who want them, and getting rid of the "work penalty" in welfare programs would encourage more people to go out looking in the first place. The minimum wage has increasingly made it difficult to have internship or apprenticeship programs that are part work and part training. That's not a big problem for wealthy or middle-class adolescents, who can invest separately in higher education programs.[5] But minimum wage laws prevent the bundling of training and work programs that have proved effective in other countries.[6] So, one BIG improvement would be the elimination of minimum wage laws.

---

[5] For a discussion of the issues presented by "unpaid internships," see Cohen (2013). By their very nature, such unpaid "work" is more feasible for young people from middle-class families because the parents can pay living expenses. Being able to pay some wages, greater than zero but less than a "living wage," would make such experiences more accessible. As is clear from the Wage and Hour Division (2010) documentation, to qualify as an internship the "work" cannot be work in any way at all. But this simply makes internships more expensive, and again rules out young people with fewer skills.

[6] Germany, in particular, has a number of well-developed apprenticeship programs that smoothly combine education and work, at wages above zero but below the "minimum" wage. See Jacoby (2014) and Winkelmann (1997).

The benefits of basic income have been heralded by some surprising scholars, including Friedman (1962), and Murray (1993). I will summarize Friedman's argument for an NIT this way.

- First, taxpayers could pay less, and the poor could receive more, for any given amount of money to be transferred. Much of the enormous apparatus of administration could be scrapped.
- Second, calculating the cost of the in-kind benefit, and then giving that benefit in cash instead, may be superior, or cannot be worse. The poor person can buy the bundle that would have been provided in kind, if in fact that is what they most prefer.
- Third, a recipient of aid is more likely to act responsibly and more carefully in allocating the funds among alternative uses. Rather than depending on the state to fulfill needs, the recipient of cash payments will rely on the state to provide means, allowing the recipients to retain the autonomy to choose what needs those means will be used to meet.

Switching from the current system to a basic income system would save money on the spending side, increase the amount received by recipients, and increase the liberty and autonomy of the recipients at the same time. We could do worse. And we almost certainly will. While a BIG is not perfect, having a safety net that recognizes the general benefits and gives citizens a sense that they are insulated from the most unpredictable effects of the new economy will make the inevitability of the coming economic revolution less disruptive.

FINAL WORDS

We are on the verge of the third great economic revolution. The only thing we know for certain is that, if this revolution works out as I have claimed, the changes it causes will be wrenching and far-reaching.

On the plus side, entrepreneurs will be able to work from anywhere, selling almost anything, *because* what they are really selling is a reduction in transaction cost. Coupled with new and innovative payment systems such as Bitcoin, the potential for middleman software is limitless. There is a debate about whether Bitcoin's key

innovation is anonymity, or pseudonymous assurance of secure transactions, but I expect the latter will turn out to be more important. The
blockchain, regardless of the currency units used to denominate
value, is a thunderbolt across the dark sky of nations that lack institutions for clearing transactions. In one step, a transaction system
based on Bitcoin can leapfrog the decades-long slog of developing
banks, a floating currency, an honest legal system, and an incorrupt-
ible police force. Entrepreneurs can work, be productive, and get paid,
in lawless failed states like Somalia or Illinois.[7]

On the darker side, people who want traditional lives may not
be able to find jobs, and ownership may become a luxury beyond the
means of all but wealthy elites. While people who are able to organize
transactions by writing software may become wealthy, people who
lack skills or interests may be shoved aside. Further, there are already
rumblings of a very different kind of sharing economy, where instead
of peer-to-peer cooperation the dominant form is specialization, with
some people buying up apartment blocks and then renting them out
on Airbnb full time. eBbay was for a decade or more a way of sharing
by reselling old stuff; now it and other online selling platforms have
come to look more like electronic malls, competing with Amazon
more than neighborhood garage sales.

But even here the darkest, most pessimistic view contains a ray
of light. Having access to triangulation (including delivery by Uber-like
driverless cars), transaction, and trust will allow a burgeoning of local
artisanal food and service providers. We already see this with extremely
high-quality boutique producers in Brooklyn and San Francisco, providing everything pickles and jams to organic produce and cured meats.
Some items, especially foods and services, cannot be rented. Having a
smart phone will help people find these providers; having software to

---

[7] As Leeson (2007) notes, the collapse of a state may make more space for
entrepreneurial activity, particularly institutional entrepreneurship, compared to a
barely functional but predatory state. Leeson considers the case of Somalia; the point
is not that Somalia is in any way a system to be emulated. It is just that (my
comparison, not Leeson's) collapse may be better than Illinois.

process the delivery and transaction will reduce the cost to the point where the providers can make a living. In twenty years, even the largest cities may once again be a collection of small villages, with local deliveries of cheese, fresh produce, and delicious and nutritious foods made straight to houses and apartments. Gone will be the days of "big box" groceries with football field-sized parking lots.

In the nineteenth century, labor costs were so low that deliveries and home services were common; in the twenty-first century, low transaction cost will take us back to a system of local deliveries, personal connections, and more variety and quality than a "one size fits all" system can deliver. The transaction costs revolution can help us share "stuff" by renting, but it can also help us reconnect with our neighborhood. And our neighbors.

I worry that the conclusions I have offered sound unduly pessimistic. And in fact I do think we are in for some difficult times, and for some people – just as was true in the Neolithic and Industrial revolutions – the quality of life may suffer, at least for a while. But there are also reasons to be optimistic. People do not really need *jobs* as much as they need an *identity*, something that they can define themselves as and form communities around. For a period of not quite 300 years, people have defined their identity as being tied up with their job but that need not be the case in the future. If I can make bourbon-basil pickles and have them delivered by a driverless car to a devoted local clientele, that may be my "job," or my identity. Perhaps I work producing things for sale, or perhaps I'm sharing part of my personal identity that happens to be delicious. The distinction may soon seem less important than it does to us now.

The coming economic revolution will leave us untethered, but untethered also means free. People will be obliged to find new meaning in their lives and new identities to organize that meaning. Kevin Kelly (2016) gives us an idea of what that might be like:

> When robots and automation do our most basic work, making it relatively easy for us to be fed, clothed, and sheltered, then we are

free to ask, "What are humans for?" Industrialization did more than
just extend the average human lifespan. It led a greater percentage
of the population to decide that humans were meant to be
ballerinas, full-time musicians, mathematicians, athletes, fashion
designers, yoga masters, fan-fiction authors, and folks with one-of-a
kind titles on their business cards. With the help of our machines,
we could take up these roles; but of course, over time, the machines
will do these as well. We'll then be empowered to dream up yet
more answers to the question "What should we do?" It will be
many generations before a robot can answer that.

(p. 57)

References

Aiméa, Carla, Guillaume Laval, Etienne Patin, Paul Verdu, Laure Ségurel, Raphaëlle Chaix, Tatyana Hegay, Luis Quintana-Murci, Evelyne Heyer, and Frédéric Austerlitz. 2013. "Human Genetic Data Reveal Contrasting Demographic Patterns between Sedentary and Nomadic Populations That Predate the Emergence of Farming." *Molecular Biology and Evolution* 30(12): 2629–2644.

Akbara, Yusaf H., and Andrea Tracognab. 2018. The sharing economy and the future of the hotel industry: Transaction cost theory and platform economics. *International Journal of Hospitality Management.* 71: 91–101.

Alaska Permanent Fund. N.d. "What Is the Alaska Permanent Fund?" www.apfc .org/home/Content/aboutFund/aboutPermFund.cfm.

Alchian, Armen. 1950. "Uncertainty, Evolution and Economic Theory." *Journal of Political Economy* 58: 211–221.

Anders, George. 2014. "Horses Lost Job Security in 1910; Are We Stuck in Their Hoof Prints?" *Forbes.* November 6. www.forbes.com/sites/georgeanders/2014/ 11/06/horses-lost-job-security-in-1910-are-we-stuck-in-their-hoofprints/#4d563 ba25571.

Anderson, Chris. 2008. *The Long Tail: Why the Future of Business Is Selling Less of More.* Revised edition. New York: Hachette Books.

Anderson, Monica. 2017. "Digital Divide Persists Even as Lower-Income Americans Make Gains in Tech Adoption." Pew Research Center. www.pewresearch .org/fact-tank/2017/03/22/digital-divide-persists-even-as-lower-income-ameri cans-make-gains-in-tech-adoption/.

Andreessen, Marc. 2011. "Software Is Eating the World." *Wall Street Journal,* August 20. A28.

Aristotle. 1979. *Politics and Poetics.* Translated by Jowett and Butcher. Norwalk, CT: Easton Press.

Asdfasdfasd. 2013. "Why a Drill Is a Bad Example for the Sharing Economy." www .credport.org/blog/12-Why-a-Drill-is-a-Bad-Example-for-the-Sharing-Economy.

Auerswald, Philip E. 2008. "Entrepreneurship in the Theory of the Firm." *Small Business Economics* 30(2): 111–126.

Ayres, Ian, Frederick E. Vars, and Nasser Zakariya. 2005. "To Insure Prejudice: Racial Disparities in Taxicab Tipping." Yale Law Faculty Scholarship Series. Paper 1232. http://digitalcommons.law.yale.edu/fss_papers/1232.

Barker, Graeme. 2009. *The Agricultural Revolution in Prehistory: Why Did Foragers Become Farmers?* New York: Oxford University Press.

Barzel, Yoram. 1982. "Measurement Cost and the Organization of Markets." *Journal of Law and Economics* 25(1): 27–48.

Bastiat, Frederic. 1848. "That Which Is Seen, and That Which Is Not Seen." Indianapolis, IN: Liberty Fund. www.econlib.org/library/Bastiat/basEss1.html.

Bastiat, Frederic, 1996. *Economics Sophisms.* New York: Foundation for Economic Education. First published in 1845.

Bessen, James. 2015. *Learning by Doing: The Real Connection between Innovation, Wages, and Wealth.* New Haven, CT: Yale University Press.

Boettke, Peter J. and Christopher J. Coyne. 2003. "Entrepreneurship and Development: Cause or Consequence?" *Advances in Austrian Economics* 6: 67–87.

Boettke, Peter J. and Christopher J. Coyne. 2009. "Context Matters: Institutions and Entrepreneurship." *Foundations and Trends in Entrepreneurship* 5(3): 135–209.

Boettke, Peter J., Christopher J. Coyne, and Peter T. Leeson. 2008. "Institutional Stickiness and the New Development Economics." *American Journal of Economics and Sociology* 67(2): 331–358.

Braidwood, Robert J. 1960. "The Agricultural Revolution." *Scientific American* 203: 130–148.

Brand, Stewart and Matt Herron. 1985. "'Keep Designing'; How the Information Economy Is Being Created and Shaped by the Hacker Ethic." *Whole Earth Review.* December 20: 47–48.

Brown, Kristen. 2015. "How Much Would It Cost Uber to Make Drivers Employees? (Hint: It's A Lot.)." *Fusion Online.* http://fusion.net/story/153243/uber-drivers-costs-if-employees/.

Brown, Kristen. 2016. "Airbnb Has Made It Nearly Impossible to Find a Place to Live in This City." *Fusion Online.* http://fusion.kinja.com/airbnb-has-made-it-nearly-impossible-to-find-a-place-to-1793856969 5/24/16.

Buchanan, James, and Yong Yoon. 2002. "*Globalization as Framed by the Two Logics of Trade.*" *The Independent Review* 6(3): 399–405.

Bureau of Labor Statistics. 2014. "Employment and Unemployment among Youth – Summer 2014." USDL-14-1498. August 13. www.bls.gov/news.release/youth.nr0.htm.

Burlington, Bo. 1989. "The Entrepreneur of the Decade: An Interview with Steven Jobs." *INC.* April 1. www.inc.com/magazine/19890401/5602.html.

Burrows, Peter, and Ronald Grover. 1998. "Steve Jobs: Movie Mogul?" *Business Week.* Nov. 23: 140–154.

Byrne, Kevin. 2016. "Snow Removal Industry Beginning to See Shift to Uber Model of On-Demand Services." *AccuWeather.* www.accuweather.com/en/weather-

news/snow-removal-industry-shifts-to-uber-like-on-demand-plow-services/
54737983.

Cairncross, Frances. 1999. *The Death of Distance: How the Communications Revolution Will Change Our Lives.* Cambridge, MA: Harvard Business Press.

California Superior Court. 2015. "Berwick vs. Uber Technologies." *Historical and Topical Legal Documents,* 985. http://digitalcommons.law.scu.edu/historical/985.

Chandler, Alfred. 1977. *The Visible Hand: The Managerial Revolution in American Business.* Cambridge, MA: Belknap–Harvard University Press.

Cheung, Steven N. S. 1969. *The Theory of Share Tenancy.* Chicago: University of Chicago Press.

Christensen, Clayton M., Michael E. Raynor, and Rory McDonald. 2015. "What Is Disruptive Innovation?" *Harvard Business Review.* December: 44–53.

Christensen, Rob. 2010. *The Paradox of Tar Heel Politics: The Personalities, Elections, and Events That Shaped Modern North Carolina.* Chapel Hill: University of North Carolina Press.

Cichon, Steve. 2014. "Everything from This 1991 Radio Shack Ad You Can Now Do with Your Phone." *The Huffington Post Blog.* January 16. www.huffingtonpost.com/steve-cichon/radio-shack-ad_b_4612973.html.

Clark, Patrick. 2014. "Hoarder Nation: America's Self-Storage Industry Is Booming." *Bloomberg News,* December 1. www.bloomberg.com/bw/articles/2014-12-01/cyber-monday-gifts-final-resting-place-self-storage.

Clarke, Roger. 1999. "Information Wants to Be Free ..." www.rogerclarke.com/II/IWtbF.html.

Coase, Ronald H. 1937. "The Nature of the Firm." *Economica* 4(16): 386–405.

Coase, Ronald H. 1960. "The Problem of Social Cost." *Journal of Law and Economics* 3: 1–44.

Coase, Ronald H. 2000. "The Acquisition of Fisher Body by General Motors." *Journal of Law & Economics* 43: 15–31.

Coase, Ronald H. 2002. *The Intellectual Portrait Series: A Conversation with Ronald H. Coase,* interviewed by Richard Epstein. Indianapolis: Liberty Fund. http://oll.libertyfund.org/titles/979.

Cohen, Steve. 2013. "Minimum Wage for Interns? It Misses the Point. Yes, I Did Unpaid Grunt Work. But Guess What: It Was Also an Invaluable Experience." *Wall Street Journal.* January 7. www.wsj.com/articles/SB10001424127887323476304578197520954865406.

Commons, J. R. 1931. "Institutional Economics." *American Economic Review* 21: 648–657.

Conda, Cesar, and Derek Khanna. 2016. "Uber for Welfare: A Bold Proposal to Use the 'Gig Economy' to Reboot the Safety Net." *Politico.* January 27.

www.politico.com/agenda/story/2016/1/uber-welfare-sharing-gig-economy-000031#ixzz3yfWmNK9i.

Cowen, Tyler. 1999. "The Costs of Cooperation." *Review of Austrian Economics* 12(2): 161–173.

Cowen, Tyler. 2011. *The Great Stagnation: How America Ate All the Low-Hanging Fruit of Modern History, Got Sick, and Will (Eventually) Feel Better.* New York: Penguin/Dutton.

Cowen, Tyler. 2013. *Average Is Over: Powering America Beyond the Age of the Great Stagnation.* New York: Penguin/Dutton.

Cowen, Tyler. 2017. *The Complacent Class: The Self-Defeating Quest for the American Dream.* New York: St. Martin's Press.

Cowen, Tyler and David Parker. 1997. *Markets in the Firm: A Market-Process Approach to Management.* London: Institute for Economic Affairs.

Coyle, Marcia. 2017. "Justices Ground Startup Flytenow, the 'Uber of the Sky': D.C. Circuit Ruling, Favoring the Federal Aviation Administration, Won't Be Reviewed." *National Law Journal.* January 9. www.law.com/nationallawjour nal/almID/1202776363942/?slreturn=20171028213236.

Davidson, Adam. 2015. "What Hollywood Can Teach Us about the Future of Work," *New York Times,* May 5.

"Defining 'Employee' in the Gig Economy." 2015. Editorial, *New York Times.* July 18. www.nytimes.com/2015/07/19/opinion/sunday/defining-employee-in-the-gig-economy.html.

Demsetz, Harold. 1966. "Some Aspect of Property Rights." *Journal of Law and Economics* 9: 61–70.

Demsetz, Harold. 1967. "A Theory of Property Rights," *American Economic Review* 57: 347–359.

Demsetz, Harold. 1969. "Information and Efficiency: Another Viewpoint." *Journal of Law and Economics* 12(1): 1-22.

Department of Health and Human Services. 2014. "2014 Poverty Guidelines: One Version of the [U.S.] Federal Poverty Measure." http://aspe.hhs.gov/poverty/14poverty.cfm.

Diamond, Jared. 1987. "The Worst Mistake in the History of the Human Race." *Discover* May: 64–66.

Diamond, Jared. 2013. *The World Until Yesterday: What Can We Learn from Traditional Societies?* New York: Penguin.

DiBona, Chris, Sam Ockman, and Mark Stone. 1999. "Introduction." *Open Sources: Voices from the Open Source Revolution.* O'Reilly Media. www.oreilly.com/openbook/opensources/book/intro.html.

Domingos, Pedro. 2016. "Machine Learning and the Master Algorithm." EconTalk Podcast. Interviewed by Russ Roberts. May 9, 2016. www.econtalk.org/arch ives/2016/05/pedro_domingos.html.

Dubnar, Robin, and Richard Sosis. 2017. "Optimising Human Community Sizes." *Evolution and Human Behavior*, 39: forthcoming.

Ducheneaut, Nicholas, and Nicholas Yee. 2009. "Collective Solitude and Social Networks in World of Warcraft." In *Social Networking Communities and E-Dating Services: Concepts and Implications*. Edited by C. Romm-Livermore and K. Setzekorn, 78–100. Hershey, PA: Information Science Reference/IGI Global.

Dunbar, R. I. M. 1992. "Neocortex Size as a Constraint on Group Size in Primates." *Journal of Human Evolution* 22(6): 469–493.

Durkheim, Emile. 1997. *Division of Labor in Society*. Florence, MA: Free Press.

"[The] Economics of Renting Vs. Owning Construction Equipment." 2017. ConExpoConAgg News. January. www.conexpoconagg.com/news/january-2017/the-economics-of-renting-vs-owning-construction-eq/.

Einav, Liran, Chiara Farronato, and Jonathan Levin. 2015. "Peer to Peer Markets." National Bureau of Economic Research, Inc. NBER Working Papers: 21496.

Ensminger, E. M. 1969. *Horses and Horsemanship*. Danville, IL: Interstate Printers and Publishers.

Feeney, Matthew. 2015. "Is Ridesharing Safe?" *Cato Policy Analysis* 767 (January 27). Washington, DC: Cato Institute. www.cato.org/blog/ridesharing-safe.

Felson, Marcus and Joe L. Spaeth. 1978. "Community Structure and Collaborative Consumption: A routine activity approach," *American Behavioral Scientist*, 21: 614–624.

Ferguson, Adam. 1996. *An Essay on the History of Civil Society*. New York: Cambridge University Press. First published in 1782.

Friedman, David. *Law's Order*. Princeton, NJ: Princeton University Press, 2000.

Friedman, Milton. 2002. *Capitalism and Freedom: Fortieth Anniversary Edition*. Chicago: University of Chicago Press. First published in 1962.

Friedman, Thomas. 2013. "Welcome to the Sharing Economy." *New York Times*. July 20. www.nytimes.com/2013/07/21/opinion/sunday/friedman-welcome-to-the-sharing-economy.html?pagewanted=all&_r=0.

Fry, Douglas P., and Patrik Söderberg. 2013. "Lethal Aggression in Mobile Forager Bands and Implications for the Origins of War." *Science* 341(6143): 270–273.

Gabriel, Mary. 2012. *Love and Capital: Karl and Jenny Marx and the Birth of a Revolution*. Boston: Back Bay Books.

Garfield, Eugene. 1983. "The Tyranny of the Horn – Automobile, That Is." *Current Comments*, 28(July 11): 5–11.

Ge, Yanbo, Christopher R. Knittel, Don MacKenzie, Stephen Zoepf. 2016. "Racial and Gender Discrimination in Transportation Network Companies." NBER Working Paper No. 22776, http://dx.doi.org/10.3386/w22776.

Gaus, Gerald. 2010. *The Order of Public Reason: A Theory of Freedom and Morality in a Diverse and Bounded World*. New York: Cambridge University Press.

George, Henry. 1951. *Progress and Poverty: An Inquiry into the Cause of Industrial Depression and of Increase of Want with Increase of Wealth*. New York: Robert Schalkenbach Foundation. First published in 1897.

Gerschenkron, Alexander. 1962. *Economic Backwardness in Historical Perspective, a Book of Essays*, Cambridge, Massachusetts: Belknap Press of Harvard University Press.

Gladwell, Malcolm. 2000. *The Tipping Point: How Little Things Can Make a Big Difference*. Boston, MA: Back Bay Books.

Goldberg, Victor. 1989. "Production Functions, Transaction Costs, and the New Institutionalism." In *Readings in the Economics of Contract Law*. Edited by Victor P. Goldberg, pp. 21–23. New York: Cambridge University Press.

Golden, Bernard. 2013. *Amazon Web Services for Dummies*. New York: For Dummies.

Goncalves B, Perra N, Vespignani A. 2011. "Modeling Users' Activity on Twitter Networks: Validation of Dunbar's Number." *PLoS ONE* 6(8): e22656.

Graaf, Johannes de Villiers. 1987. "Lump Sum Taxes." In *The New Palgrave: A Dictionary of Economics*. Vol. 3, 251–252. New York: Palgrave-Macmillan.

Graham, Daniel A., Edward Jacobson and E. Roy Weintraub. 1972. "Transactions Costs and the Convergence of a "Trade Out of Equilibrium" Adjustment Process." *International Economic Review*. 13(1): 123–131.

Greene, Ann Norton. 2008. *Horses at Work: Harnessing Power in Industrial America*. Cambridge, MA: Harvard University Press.

Griffin, Emma. 2014. *Liberty's Dawn: A People's History of the Industrial Revolution*. New Haven: Yale University Press.

GSMA Intelligence. 2014. "ANALYSIS–Understanding 5G: Perspectives on Future Technological Advancements in Mobile." Groupe Speciale Mobile Association. www.gsmaintelligence.com/research/?file=141208-5g.pdf&download.

Guzman, Ricardo, and Michael Munger. "Euvoluntariness and Just Market Exchange: Moral Dilemmas from Locke's 'Venditio.'" *Public Choice* 158: 39–49.

Harari, Yuval Noah. 2015. *Sapiens: A Brief History of Humankind*. New York: Harper.

Hardin, Garrett. 1968. "The Tragedy of the Commons." *Science* 162(3859): 1243–1248.

Harris, P. G. S. 2003. *The History of Human Populations: Migration, Urbanization, and Structural Change*. Santa Barbara, CA: Greenwood Press.

Hicks, John. 1969. *A Theory of Economic History*. Oxford: Oxford University Press.

Hof, Robert. 2016. "Ten Years Later Amazon Web Services Defies the Skeptics." *Forbes*. www.forbes.com/sites/roberthof/2016/03/22/ten-years-later-amazon-web-services-defies-skeptics/#1df9fb776c44.

Horton, John J., and Richard Zeckhauser. 2016. "Owning, Using and Renting: Some Simple Economics of the 'Sharing Economy'" NEBER Working Paper 22029. www.nber.org/papers/w22029.

Hume, David. 2004. "Of the Origin of Justice and Property." *Treatise of Human Nature*. Reprinted as *The Philosophical Works of David Hume. Including all the Essays, and exhibiting the more important Alterations and Corrections in the successive Editions by the Author*. Reprint. Chestnut Hill, MA: Adamant Media Corporation. First published in 1740.

Hummell, Jeffrey. 2001. "The Will to Be Free: The Role of Ideology in National Defense." *Independent Review* 5(4): 523–537.

Hutt, William H. 1940. "The Concept of Consumers' Sovereignty." *The Economic Journal* 50(197): 66–77.

Jacoby, Tamar. 2014. "Why Germany Is So Much Better at Training Its Workers." *The Atlantic*. October 16. www.theatlantic.com/business/archive/2014/10/why-germany-is-so-much-better-at-training-its-workers/381550/.

Jaffe, Erik. 2014. "Why New Yorkers Can't Find a Taxi When It Rains." *CityLab*. www.citylab.com/environment/2014/10/why-new-yorkers-cant-find-a-taxi-when-it-rains/381652/.

Jardim, Ekaterina, Mark C. Long, Robert Plotnick, Emma van Inwegen, Jacob Vigdor, and Hilary Wething. 2017. "Minimum Wage Increases, Wages, and Low-Income Employment: Evidence from Seattle." Cambridge, MA: National Bureau of Economic Research. Working Paper 23532. www.nber.org/papers/w23532.

Kalanick, Travis. 2010. "Uber's Founding." https://newsroom.uber.com/ubers-founding/.

Karolevitz, Robert F. 1968. *This Was Pioneer Motoring: An Album of Nostalgic Automobilia*. Seattle: Superior Publishing Co.

Keeley, Lawrence. 1997. *War before Civilization: The Myth of the Peaceful Savage*. Oxford: Oxford University Press.

Kelly, Kevin. 2016. *The Inevitable: Understanding the 12 Technological Forces That Will Shape Our Future*, New York: Viking Press.

Keynes, John Maynard. 1962. *Essays in Persuasion*. Revised edition. New York: W. W. Norton & Co.

Khaldun, Ibn. 2015. *The Muqaddimah: An Introduction to History*. Edited by N. J. Dawood. Translated by Franz Rosenthal. Princeton: Princeton University Press.

Kirzner, Israel. 1971. "Entrepreneurship & the Market Approach to Development." In *Toward Liberty: Essays in Honor of Ludwig von Mises on the Occasion of his 90th Birthday*. Edited by F. A. Hayek et al. Menlo Park: Institute for Humane Studies.

Kirzner, Israel. 1973. *Competition and Entrepreneurship*. Chicago: University of Chicago Press.

Kirzner, Israel. 1979. *Perception, Opportunity and Profit: Studies in the Theory of Entrepreneurship*. Chicago: University of Chicago Press.

Kirzner, Israel. 2011. *Market Theory and the Price System*. Edited by Peter J. Boettke and Frédéric Sautet. Indianapolis: Liberty Fund. First published in 1963.

Kloberdanz, Kristin. 2014. "Taxi Drivers: Years of Living Dangerously." *HealthDay*. March 11. http://consumer.healthday.com/encyclopedia/work-and-health-41/occupational-healthnews-507/taxi-drivers-years-of-living-dangerously-646377.html.

Konrad, Kai. 2009. "Investing in regimes with stationary or roving bandits." In *Guns and Butter: The Economic Causes and Consequences of Conflict*. Edited by D. Hess, 99–121. Cambridge, MA: MIT Press.

Koopman, Christopher, and Eli Dourado. 2017. "An Easy Way to Make the Skies Friendlier: Elaine Chao could open the way to ride-sharing for planes." *Wall Street Journal*, March 15, A28. www.wsj.com/articles/an-easy-way-to-make-the-skies-friendlier-1489618294

Koopman, Christopher. 2015. "Opportunity and Mobility in the Sharing Economy." *Real Clear Technology*. May 19. www.realcleartechnology.com/articles/2015/05/19/opportunity_and_mobility_in_the_sharing_economy_1250.html.

Krause, Paul. 1992. *The Battle for Homestead, 1880–1892: Politics, Culture, and Steel*. Pittsburgh: University of Pittsburgh Press.

Kropotkin, Piotr. 2009. *Mutual Aid: A Factor of Evolution*. London: Freedom Press. First published in 1902.

Kuhn, Peter J., and Fernando Lozano. 2008. The Expanding Workweek? Understanding Trends in Long Work Hours among U.S. Men, 1979–2004." *Journal of Labor Economics* 26(2): 311–343.

Kurrild-Klitgaard, Peter, and Gert Tinggaard Svendsen. 2003. "Rational Bandits: Plunder, Public Goods and the Vikings." *Public Choice* 117: 255–272.

Laet, Siegfried (de). 1994. "From the First Food Production to the First States." In *History of Humanity: Prehistory and the Beginning of Civilization*. Vol. 1 361–372. Edited by SJ de Leon et al. New York: Unesco/Taylor and Francis.

Lamberton, Cait Poynor, and Randall L. Rose, 2012. "When Is Ours Better Than Mine? A Framework for Understanding and Altering Participation in Commercial Sharing Systems." *Journal of Marketing* 76(4): 109–125.

Landes, David S. 1969. *The Unbound Prometheus: Technological Change and Industrial Development in Western Europe from 1750 to the Present*. Cambridge and New York: Press Syndicate of the University of Cambridge.

Langlois, Richard. "Transaction Cost Economics in Real Time." *Industrial and Corporate Change* 1:99–127.

Leeson, Peter. 2007. "Better Off Stateless: Somalia before and after Government Collapse." *Journal of Comparative Economics* 35(4): 689–710.

Leeson, Peter, and Peter Boettke. 2009. "Two-Tiered Entrepreneurship and Economic Development." *International Review of Law and Economics* 29(3), 252–259.

Levitt, Theodore. 1960. Marketing Myopia. *Harvard Business Review* 38(4): 45–56.

Levy, Stephen. 2011. "Jeff Bezos Owns the Web in More Ways Than You Think." *Wired.* www.wired.com/2011/11/ff_bezos/.

Leys, Simon. 1986. *The Burning Forest: Essays on Chinese Culture and Politics.* New York: Holt, Rinehart, and Winston.

Locke, John. 1948. *The Second Treatise of Civil Government and a Letter Concerning Toleration.* Oxford: B. Blackwell. First published in 1692.

Lucas, Robert. 1979. "Sharing, Monitoring, and Incentives: Marshallian Misallocation Reassessed." *Journal of Political Economy* 87(3): 501–521.

Lucas, Robert E., Jr. 2002. *Lectures on Economic Growth.* Cambridge, MA: Harvard University Press.

Mandeville, Bernard. 2016. *The Fable of the Bees.* Düsseldorf: Verlag Press.

Manuscript Cotton Tiberius A, part 3 is a reference to a fragment of an eleventh-century psalter, probably produced at Christchurch, Canterbury.

Marx, Karl. 1992. *Capital: 3 Volumes.* Translated by Ben Fowkes. London: Penguin Books.

Marx, Karl. 2012. *Economic and Philosophical Manuscripts of 1844.* North Chelmsford, MA: Courier Corporation.

McGauley, Joe, and Daniel Cole. 2016. "The European Hitchhiking App That Beats the Hell Out of Uber. *The Thrillest: Tech.* June 24. www.thrillist.com/tech/nation/blablacar-ride-sharing-apps-hitchhiking-road-trips.

Meyer, Jared. 2016a. "Uber for Planes." *Forbes.* May 31. www.forbes.com/sites/jaredmeyer/2016/05/31/uber-for-planes/

Meyer, Jared. 2016b. *Uber-Positive: Why Americans Love the Sharing Economy.* Encounter Books.

Mindell, David A. 2015. *Our Robots, Ourselves: Robotics and the Myths of Autonomy.* New York: Viking Press/Random House.

Mises, Ludwig (von). 1952. "Profit and Loss." *Planning for Freedom.* South Holland, Ill.: Libertarian Press.

Mises, Ludwig (von). 2007. *Bureaucracy.* Edited by Bettina Bien Greaves. Indianapolis: Liberty Fund. http://oll.libertyfund.org/titles/1891. First published in 1944.

Monceau, Henri-Louis Duhamel (du). 2016. *Art de l'Épinglier* (The Art of the Pin-Maker). Pamphlet. Published for M. de Reaumur. New Delhi: Gyan Books. First published in 1761.

Molinari, Gustave de. *The Production of Security*. Translated by J. H. McCulloch. Auburn, AL: Ludwig von Mises Institute, 2009. First published in 1849.

Mukherjee, Siddhartha. 2017. "A.I. vs. M.D.: What Happens When Diagnosis Is Automated?" *New Yorker*. April 3. www.newyorker.com/magazine/2017/04/03/ai-versus-md.

Munger, Michael. 2008. "Bosses Don't Wear Bunny Slippers: If Markets Are So Great, Why Are There Firms?" Indianapolis: Liberty Fund. www.econlib.org/library/Columns/y2008/Mungerfirms.html

Munger, Michael. 2009. "Middlemen: Market-makers or Parasites?" Indianapolis: Liberty Fund. www.econlib.org/library/Columns/y2009/Mungermiddlemen.html.

Munger, Michael. 2011. "'Basic Income' Is Not an Obligation, But It Might Be a Legitimate Choice." *Basic Income Studies* 6(2): 1–13.

Munger, Michael. 2015a. "Sabotaging Uber: The Umpire Strikes Back." *Foundation for Economic Education*, June 23. https://fee.org/articles/sabotaging-uber-the-umpire-strikes-back

Munger, Michael. 2015b. "Editor's Introduction" (485–488) and "One and One-Half Cheers for BIG" (503–514), *Independent Review*. 20(1). www.independent.org/publications/tir/toc.asp?issueID=81

Murray, Charles. 2006. *In Our Hands: A Plan to Replace the Welfare State*. Washington, DC: AEI Press.

Murray, Charles. 2012. *Coming Apart: The State of White America, 1960–2010*. New York: Crown Publishing Group.

North, Douglass. 1981. *Structure and Change in Economic History*. New York: Norton.

North, Douglass. 1990. *Institutions, Institutional Change, and Economic History*. New York: Cambridge University Press.

North, Douglass, John Joseph Wallis, and Barry Weingast. 2009. *Violence and Social Orders: A Conceptual Framework for Interpreting Recorded Human History*. New York: Cambridge University Press.

Nye, John. 2017. "Your Neighbor's Fancy Car Should Make You Feel Better About Income Inequality." *Reason*. 49(3): 42–47. http://reason.com/archives/2017/06/18/your-neighbors-fancy-car-shoul

Occupational Safety and Health Administration, 2000. Risk Factors and Protective Measures for Taxi and Livery Drivers. U.S. Department of Labor. www.osha.gov/OSHAFacts/taxi-livery-drivers.pdf.

O'Driscoll, Gerald P., and Mario Rizzo. 1996. *The Economics of Time and Ignorance*. New York: Routledge Press.

Olson, Mancur. *The Logic of Collective Action*. 1965. Cambridge, MA: Harvard University Press.

Olson, Mancur. 1982. *The Rise and Decline of Nations: Economic Growth, Stagflation, and Social Rigidities*. New Haven, CT: Yale University Press.

Olson, Mancur. 1993. "Dictatorship, Democracy, and Development." *American Political Science Review* 87(3): 567–576.

Olson, Mancur. *Power and Prosperity: Outgrowing Communist and Capitalist Dictatorships*. London: Oxford University Press, 2000.

Olson, Mancur, and Martin McGuire. 1996. "The Economics of Autocracy and Majority Rule: The Invisible Hand and the Use of Force." *Journal of Economic Literature* 34(1): 72–96.

Open Source Initiative, n.d. "The Open Source Definition (Annotated) (version 1.9)." https://opensource.org/osd-annotated.

Paine, Thomas. 1795. *Agrarian Justice*. Pamphlet. www.thomas-painefriends.org/paine-thomas_agrarian-justice-1795-01.html.

Pethokoukis, James. 2016. "What the Story of ATMs and Bank Tellers Reveals about the 'Rise of the Robots' and Jobs." American Enterprise Institute. www.aei.org/publication/what-atms-bank-tellers-rise-robots-and-jobs/

Queenan, Joe. 2017. "A Sharing Economy for Pants, Hats and More Car rides Were Just the Beginning; Communal Egg Whisks, Anyone?" *Wall Street Journal*. July 13. www.wsj.com/articles/a-sharing-economy-for-pants-hats-and-more-1499960124.

Radford, R. A. 1945. "The Economic Organisation of a P.O.W. Camp. *Economica*, 12(48): 189–201.

Reinhardt, Andy. 1998. "Interview with Steve Jobs." *BusinessWeek*. May 25. 3579: 62–64.

Richman, Dan. 2016. "Amazon without AWS? Online Retailer Would Have Posted Big Loss If Not for Booming Cloud Business." *Geekwire*. October 31. www.geekwire.com/2016/amazon-without-aws-online-retailer-posted-big-loss-not-booming-cloud-business/.

Ridley, Matt. 2011. *The Rational Optimist: How Prosperity Evolves*. New York: Harper and Row Publishing.

Rifkin, Jeremy. 2014. *The Zero Marginal Cost Society: The Internet of Things, the Collaborative Commons, and the Eclipse of Capitalism*. New York: Palgrave, Macmillan.

Rizzo, Mario. 1996. "Time and Ignorance after Ten Years." In *The Economics of Time and Ignorance*. Second edition. Edited by Mario Rizzo and Gerald O'Driscoll, pp. xi–xxix. London and New York: Routledge.

Rizzo, Mario, and Gerald O'Driscoll, editors. 1996. *The Economics of Time and Ignorance*. Second edition. London and New York: Routledge.

Rostow, Walt Whitman. 1960. *The Stages of Economic Growth: A Non-Communist Manifesto*. New York: Cambridge University Press.

Rousseau, Jean Jacques. 1754. *A Discourse on a Subject Proposed by the Academy of Dijon: What Is the Origin of Inequality Among Men, and Is It Authorized by Natural Law?* Translated by G. D. H. Cole. www.constitution.org/jjr/ineq.htm.

Rude, Emelyn. 2017. "The Very Short History of Food Stamp Fraud in America." *Time*. March 30. http://time.com/4711668/history-food-stamp-fraud/.

Ryan, John. 1977. *The Agricultural Economy of Manitoba Hutterite Colonies*. Toronto: McClelland and Stewart.

Say, Jean-Baptiste. 1855. *A Treatise on Political Economy: Or the Production, Distribution and Consumption of Wealth Paperback*. C. R. Prinsep, translator, and Clement C. Biddle, editor. 6$^\text{th}$ Edition. Philadelphia, PA: Lippincott, Grambo & Co.

Schneider, Henrique. 2017. *Creative Destruction and the Sharing Economy: Uber As Disruptive Innovation*. Northampton, MA: Edward Elgar Publishing.

Schumpeter, Joseph. 1934. *The Theory of Economic Development: An Inquiry into Profits, Capital, Credit, Interest, and the Business Cycle*. Cambridge, MA: Harvard University Press.

Schumpeter, Joseph. 1942. *Capitalism, Socialism, and Democracy*. Third edition. New York: Harper.

Scott, James C. 2010. *The Art of Not Being Governed: An Anarchist History of Upland Southeast Asia*. New Haven, CT: Yale University Press.

Selgin, George, and Lawrence White. 1994. "How Would the Invisible Hand Handle Money?" *Journal of Economic Literature* 32: 1718–1749.

Shackle, G. L. S. 1969. *Decision, Time, and Order in Human Affairs*. New York: Cambridge University Press.

Shackle, G. L. S. 1970. *Expectation, Enterprise and Profit: The Theory of the Firm*. Abingdon-on-Thames: Routledge.

Shavel, Michael, Sebastian Vanderzeil, and Emma Currier. 2017. "Retail Automation: Stranded Workers? Opportunities and Risks for Labor and Automation." Cornerstone Capital Group. https://cornerstonecapinc.com/2017/05/retail-automation-stranded-workers-opportunities-and-risks-for-labor-and-automation/.

Sivak, Michael, and Brandan Schoettle. 2016. "Recent Decreases in the Proportion of Persons with a Driver's License, Across All Age Groups." In *UMTRI-2016-4*, *Transportation Research Institute*. Ann Arbor: University of Michigan Press.

Skaperdas, Stergios. 1992. "Cooperation, Conflict, and Power in the Absence of Property Rights." *American Economic Review* 82: 720–739.

Skaperdas, Stergios. 2001. "The Political Economy of organized Crime: Providing Protection When the State Does Not." *Economics of Governance* 2(3): 173–202.

Smith, Adam. 1981. *An Inquiry Into the Nature and Causes of the Wealth of Nations*. Indianapolis, IN: Liberty Fund. Originally published in 1776.

Song of Insects. 2017. "Biology of Insect Song." http://songsofinsects.com/biology-of-insect-song.

Stigler, George. 1951. "The Division of Labor Is Limited by the Extent of the Market." *Journal of Political Economy* 59(3): 185–193.

Strossjan, Randall. 2010. "Failing Like a Buggy Whip Maker? Better Check Your Simile." *New York Times*, January 9. www.nytimes.com/2010/01/10/business/10digi.html.

Suellentrop, Chris. 2010. "Abandon Ownership!" *Wired* 18(11): 33.

Sundararajan, Arun. 2016. *The Sharing Economy*. Cambridge, MA: MIT Press.

Tanner, Michael. 2012. "The American Welfare State: How We Spend Nearly $1 Trillion a Year Fighting Poverty – and Fail." Cato Policy Report #694. www.cato.org/sites/cato.org/files/pubs/pdf/PA694.pdf.

Thierer, Adam. 2014. *Permissionless Innovation: The Continuing Case for Comprehensive Technological Freedom*. Arlington, VA: Mercatus Institute.

Thompson, Derek. 2015. "A World without Work." *Atlantic Monthly*. July/August. www.theatlantic.com/magazine/archive/2015/07/world-without-work/395294/.

Turner, Sharon. 1836. *The History of the Anglo-Saxons*. Sixth edition. London, England: Longman, Rees, Orme, Brown, Green, and Longman.

Uber. N.d. "Uber Community Guidelines." Uber Technologies, Inc. www.uber.com/legal/community-guidelines/us-en/

United Nations, 2013. "Deputy UN Chief Calls for Urgent Action to Tackle Global Sanitation Crisis." March 21. www.un.org/apps/news/story.asp?NewsID=44452&Cr=sanitation&Cr1=#.V0Hj6pErKUl

Van Doren, Peter. 2014. "Should Taxi Medallion Owners Be Compensated?" Cato Institute, Washington, DC. www.cato.org/blog/should-taxi-medallion-owners-be-compensated.

Vany, Arthur S. De. 1975. "Capacity Utilization under Alternative Regulatory Restraints: An Analysis of Taxi Markets." *Journal of Political Economy* 83(1): 83–94.

Vigna, Paul, and Michael Casey. 2015. *The Age of Cryptocurrency*. New York: St. Martin's Press.

Von Hayek, Friedrich Auguste. 1945. "The Use of Knowledge in Society." *American Economic Review* 35(4): 519–530.

Von Hayek, Friedrich Auguste. 1960. *The Constitution of Liberty*. Chicago: University of Chicago Press.

Von Hayek, Friedrich Auguste. 2002. "Competition as a Discovery Procedure." *The Quarterly Journal of Austrian Economics* 5(3): 9–23.

Wachowski, Lana, and Lilly Wachowski, dirs. 1999. *The Matrix*. Burbank, CA: Warner Bros. Pictures.

Wage and Hour Division. 2010. "Fact Sheet #71: Internship Programs under The Fair Labor Standards Act." U.S. Department of Labor. www.dol.gov/whd/regs/compliance/whdfs71.htm.

Wang, Ray. 2015. "Walkman to iPod: Business-Model Transformation Samsung Wants to Be Apple. And It Could Be." *Recode*. September 3. www.recode.net/2015/9/3/11618292/book-excerpt-business-model-transformation.

Warstler, Morgan. 2014. "Guaranteed Income and Choose Your Own Boss: Uber for Welfare." *Medium*. https://medium.com/@morganwarstler/guaranteed-income-choose-your-boss-1d068ac5a205#.ue6z3djcw.

Weber, Max. 1921. "Politics as a Vocation" (Politik als Beruf). *Gesammelte Politische Schriften* (Muenchen): 396–450.

Weber, Max. 1968. *Economy and Society*. Edited by Guenther Roth and Claus Wittich. Berkeley: University of California Press.

White, Sarah. 2016. "Welcome to the Gig Economy." *CIO*. www.cio.com/article/3037004/careers-staffing/hiring-trends-for-2016-welcome-to-the-gig-economy.html.

Widerquist, Karl, and Michael W. Howard. 2012. *Exporting the Alaska Model: Adapting the Permanent Fund Dividend for Reform around the World*. New York: Palgrave Macmillan.

Wilson, Edward O. 2015. *The Meaning of Human Existence*. New York: Liveright Press.

Willet, Megan. 2016. "I Spent $150 a Month Renting Clothes, And Now I'm Never Going Back to Fast Fashion." *Tech Insider*. www.businessinsider.com/rent-the-runway-unlimited-subscription-2016-4.

Williamson, Kevin D. 2013. *The End Is Near and It's Going to Be Awesome: How Going Broke Will Leave America Richer, Happier, and More Secure*. New York: Harper-Collins.

Williamson, Oliver E. 1975. *Markets and Hierarchies*. New York: Free Press.

Williamson, Oliver E. 1985. *The Economic Institutions of Capitalism: Firms, Markets, Relational Contracting*. New York: Free Press.

Winkelmann, Rainer. 1997. "How Young Workers Get Their Training: A Survey of Germany versus the United States." *Journal of Population Economics*, 10(2): 159–170.

Worstall, Tim. 2013. "An Unconditional Basic Income Is the Solution but the Important Word Here Is Basic." *Forbes*. July 12. www.forbes.com/sites/timwor

stall/2013/07/12/an-unconditional-basic-income-is-the-solution-but-the-import ant-word-here-is-basic/.

Wright, Joshua. 2013. "The Average Manufacturing Establishment Is Smaller Than You Think, and Getting Smaller." *Economic Modeling, EMSI*. April 24. www .economicmodeling.com/2013/04/24/the-average-manufacturing-establishment- is-smaller-than-you-think-and-getting-smaller/.

Zak, Paul. 2011. "Moral Markets." *Journal of Economic Behavior & Organization* 77: 212–233.

Index